BUSINESS
ETIQUETTE

The Insider's Guide to
Workplace Courtesy
and Customs

by Tim Rayborn

13-digit ISBN: 978-1-73251-269-6
10-digit ISBN: 1-73251-269-8

This book may be ordered by mail from the publisher. Please include $5.99 for postage and handling. Please support your local bookseller first!

Books published by Whalen Book Works are available at special discounts when purchased in bulk. For more information, please email us at info@whalenbookworks.com.

Whalen Book Works
68 North Street
Kennebunkport, ME 04046

www.whalenbookworks.com

Cover and interior design by Melissa Gerber
Typography: Adobe Caslon, Avenir 35 Light, Avenir 85 Heavy, Gotham, DIN, Symbol Medium and Fontbox Boathouse

Printed in China
1 2 3 4 5 6 7 8 9 0

First Edition

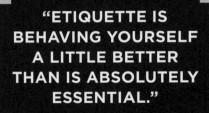

"ETIQUETTE IS
BEHAVING YOURSELF
A LITTLE BETTER
THAN IS ABSOLUTELY
ESSENTIAL."

—WILL CUPPY

CONTENTS

INTRODUCTION

This book is for those who are about to embark on new careers after graduating college, or for those maybe making a career shift after being at a previous job, especially from a very different kind of work environment. It will help you navigate the sometimes tricky world of office politics and culture, and give you the tools you need to survive and thrive. While the focus here is on the "classic" concept of a workplace: the office, the dress code, the hierarchies, the forty-hour week, etc., the advice given can be applied to any number of different workplace environments, because at its heart, business etiquette is about courtesy, respect, professionalism, and just getting along well with others, qualities that every kind of job values and that are just as important in your nonworking life.

Much of the advice that follows may seem like simple common sense, and it is. But it's also important to remind ourselves of it from time to time, and to continue to learn and update what we know and how we act around others. Some behaviors that might have been acceptable twenty years ago, no longer are. The workplace landscape is constantly evolving to accommodate shifts in culture and even the law. On the other hand, some modes of conduct are timeless and will always be appreciated. This book will teach you about both.

The book is divided into chapters covering related topics, with each offering a list of important concepts to keep in mind and learn more about. It provides a quick reference and handy guide when you want to look up something about a specific subject. Obviously, these entries are only brief summaries, but you can use them as starting points for further research into greater detail.

It should clear here that this book is not a substitute for legal, medical, or psychological advice, and if you need further help from a licensed professional on any of the topics here, you will need to seek it out. The Resources section (page 164) provides some helpful further reading, as well as websites for detailed information on such topics as discrimination, employment rights, and so on.

Entering the workplace can seem overwhelming and even frightening if you've only been a student up until now, or if your work experience has been in a field other than the standard office setting. This book will help ease some of those fears and ensure that you not only give your best at your new job but also are open to receiving experiences that are enriching, rewarding, good for your career, and maybe even fun.

CHAPTER 1

DAY-TO-DAY IN THE WORKPLACE

Your day-to-day experience in your company will vary widely depending on what kind of organization you're working for. It may be formal and traditional with cubicles and desks, and skirts and suits, or maybe it's very laid-back, with beanbags and open workspaces, and sandals and T-shirts. This is potentially new territory that can be unfamiliar and maybe even a bit intimidating, if not outright frightening. But fear not! In this chapter, you'll read about everything you need to know to navigate your surroundings with confidence.

DRESSING FOR SUCCESS

Traditionally, there was a strict, gendered dress code at most businesses. In recent decades, these rules have been relaxed somewhat, but what is considered appropriate varies widely from company to company and industry to industry. A Wall Street investment brokerage will have a drastically different look than a phone-app company in San Francisco. You'll want to ensure that you match the standards set by your company, so here are some useful guidelines.

- **Your hiring company will most likely tell you the dress code from the outset,** and if they don't, you can probably get a good sense of it just by looking around. Don't hesitate to ask! Your shorts and sandals won't fly in an established accounting firm, but pencil skirts and three-piece suits probably aren't necessary in a Seattle hemp product company. *Always* make sure you know what is expected of you before your first day!

- **Investing in appropriate clothing may seem inconvenient,** but it's just part of the job. If you need a suit, you need a suit. Also, a little more formal is almost always better than a little too casual. The term "business casual" means different things to different companies. Always ask.

- **Personal hygiene is obviously a must.** Keep your clothing and yourself clean. Extra showers and laundry are going to become a regular thing from now on. But think of the effect on others and on yourself: Do you want to be sitting next to someone who hasn't bathed in four days? Exactly.

- **With that in mind, go easy on scents.** Some people are very sensitive to them, and some workplaces outright ban them. If you don't know the policy, ask. If someone can smell your perfume or cologne from more than a foot or two away, you're probably wearing too much. And if someone *is* only a foot away from you, you might need to read the sections on office romances or harassment in chapter 4 (page 104).

- **Personal appearance guidelines vary widely from company to company.** A more traditional company may require men to keep their hair short and women to keep theirs tied back, for example. A more easygoing company may be fine with its men sporting ponytails. If you're a man with a beard, keep it clean and well-trimmed.

- **An important note:** Some cultures, ethnicities, and religions have certain requirements or accepted practices about the way hair is worn or covered, facial hair, specific articles of clothing, etc. It is not permissible for a company to discriminate against someone because of this. If you feel that your workplace is discriminating against you due to your cultural or religious practices, or you haven't been hired because of them, see Your Legal Rights and Recourses in chapter 4.

Basically, follow your company's dress guidelines and keep clean. It's really no more difficult than that.

ALL ABOUT DRESS CODES

Dress codes vary widely from company to company, from quite formal to "whatever, wear what you want!" Work dress codes are often broken down into four types, which are listed below in descending order of dressiness. Even within these categories, your particular company may have its own specific requirement, or not. These terms will give you an idea of what's expected if you hear them at an interview, an orientation, or any similar context.

- **Business Formal.** Think prestigious law firms, Wall Street companies, executive board meetings ("bored" meetings?), and everything that goes with them. This is the most formal way to dress and generally is expected of people with high-paying, executive jobs and the like. For both women and men, clothing will be sharp and probably expensive. Colors will be dark, gray, or neutral, and accompanied by white buttoned shirts, simple accents, and conservative haircuts (men's hair worn short, women's tied back). Women will be expected not to wear short skirts; pantsuits are usually quite acceptable. Business formal can also include black-tie wear to special events, such as dinners, awards, charity events, and so on.

- **Business Professional.** One step down from Business Formal, you will still be expected to be nicely dressed and well-groomed. The majority of so-called traditional office jobs have probably fallen into this category. You may have the option of less formal suits and more casual coats and jackets and might be able to inject a bit more color or patterns into your wardrobe—but check with your company to see if there are any specific restrictions.

11

- **Business Casual.** This is increasingly one of the most common dress codes, but its definitions can vary pretty widely from company to company, so you'll have to check with your HR department or other source of information to find out exact what they mean by it; it's always good to be sure! Men might not need to wear ties, but may still be expected to wear a buttoned-up shirt, and may sport khakis and such, rather than business suits. Women will likely not need anything too "suit-like" and will be able to wear more color and accents.

- **Casual.** Casual means casual, but not slobbish! Quality jeans and clean shirts of all kinds may be fine, denim skirts and colorful accents are usually good, but be aware that you still want to present well and reflect well on your company. Unless the dress code specifically states that sweatpants and T-shirts are fine, you should err on the side of a little more formal in your casual choices. You're not sitting on your couch eating chips and watching TV, after all. Or maybe you're lucky enough and that is your job?

- **Additional considerations:**

  - **Tattoos and piercings.** An increasing number of people have them, which is fine for personal expression, but you may run into some difficulties in more conservative work environments. If your job is more formal, it's best, at least initially, to keep tattoos covered: long-sleeved shirts and pants. In contrast, a casual workplace may have no restrictions. With piercings, other than women having pierced ears, you may well be expected to remove them (nose, lip, eyebrow, etc.) during work hours. Sorry, but more traditional companies probably won't accommodate you, and they have the right to ask you to do it!

- **Some other things to remember about personal appearance.** In less formal work situations, certain expectations may be relaxed: men might be able to wear longer hair in a ponytail, women or men might be able to have their hair dyed an unusual color, etc. You will need to check with you company's specific guidelines. Bear in mind that the line between dress code requirements and discrimination can be a murky one. No one can tell a Sikh man that he must remove his turban, or a Muslim woman that she needs to take off her headscarf, for example. If you find yourself coming up against this kind of discrimination, refer to chapter 4, Workplace Difficulties, for more information on how to handle the problem.

One final note:

Dress codes are an increasingly murky and mixed area, and what's fine in one place might well be forbidden in another. It's essential that you find you what, if any, codes your workplace enforces and be ready from day one to honor them.

HOW TO NEVER BE LATE

Being on time is one of those things that some people are great at. And then there are the rest of us. Still, we all acknowledge that punctuality is a good trait and we appreciate when people show up on time for something that is important to us, so what better reason for us to give back the same courtesy? Obviously, your employer expects you to be at work at a designated time, and if you show up too late, too often, you won't be there for very long. If you're someone who has problems with time management, what can you do? Here are a few ideas:

- **Accept that you're being paid to be at your workplace at a specific time.** This is a part of the job and goes with the salary you're getting. This also goes for workplace activities, such as meetings. Arriving a few minutes early is always a good practice.

- **If you have to commute to work, budget your time accordingly.** Obviously, sometimes a bus will be late, a train will be delayed, or there will be a traffic jam on the roads, and you can't always prepare for everything (just call your workplace and let them know). But make a plan and stick with it. One good rule of thumb is to add 25 percent more time than you think you'll need to get somewhere, or than what your app tells you.

- **Get up early enough so that you don't feel rushed in the mornings.** Arriving to work feeling frazzled is not a good way to start the day.

- **On the other side, please don't neglect your sleep.** Make sure you get to bed early enough to allow for a good six hours or more. Unfortunately, there is a culture of "you can sleep when you're dead" that has grown up in some businesses and industries, but this is not only unhealthy in the long run, it's potentially dangerous now. If you do suffer from sleep issues or disorders, there are many good treatments available.

- **Minimize your morning worries.** If you have trouble with early mornings (and it's pretty common!), get everything ready and laid out (your clothing, lunch, work materials, keys, etc.) the night before.

- **Set your clock or phone few minutes ahead, say five to seven minutes.** This gives you a little push, but also builds in a small amount of time as a safety when you're stumbling around in the morning.

- **Try an alarm that wakes you a bit more gently,** rather than something that blasts you awake. These can be helpful over time in adjusting sleep patterns.

- **Try a time-tracking and management app.** There are many good ones out there, so download one or more and try them out. These are useful for anything that requires you to be somewhere or do something at a specific time.

- **Set reminders on your phone for meetings and other important things** far enough in advance (say fifteen minutes before a meeting) so you can be present and fully prepared.

Everyone struggles with time management at some point. But with a little effort, you can shift those struggles into a system that works for you and keeps everyone happy.

SEVEN POINTS ABOUT PERSONAL BEHAVIOR AND ITS EFFECTS ON WORK

When you are in an office environment, you are obviously working around others; that's kind of the whole point. The presence of other people automatically means that we may have to modify some of our behaviors. Those bad habit and things we might do on our own (and let's be honest, we all do them!) need to be left at the door. It should seem obvious, but here are some general ideas for how to be on your best and most professional behavior. If you do run into problems, please see chapter 4, which offers up great advice on how to deal with any number of coworker difficulties you might encounter.

1. **First and foremost, simply be respectful of other people:** their space, their opinions, their time, and whatever they might be sensitive to. You don't need to feel as if you're walking around on eggshells, but the golden rule always applies: Treat others as you would wish to be treated. Stick with this, and a lot of problems will never come up.

2. **You may well be working with people from many different backgrounds:** cultural, political, religious, and so on. You're all there for a common purpose (the job), and that's where you need to focus. If someone holds views very different from your own? That's not relevant. Can they do their job? That is.

3. **Make sure to engage with each person** (such as in meetings) and work with their specific strengths. Understand that their expertise may be different than yours.

4. **Try to get a sense of what your coworkers' comfort levels and boundaries are.** You may be comfortable with one level of intimacy (handshakes, patting someone on the shoulder, etc.), but they are not. If in doubt, ask.

5. **Always avoid vulgarities.** Obviously, bad language and crude jokes or any humor that targets another group is never acceptable. Don't engage in these, and if you see someone who is doing so, take actions to put a stop to it. See chapter 4.

6. **Other things like belching and worse are completely uncalled for.** For obvious reasons.

7. **Basic courtesy and respect never go out of style.** Some workplace environments are more casual than others. "Read the room" and get a sense for what is acceptable. Treat your coworkers as human beings, even if not all of them are your friends, and you'll do well.

Your personal behavior reflects on you and on the company, so always mind your manners and you'll probably find that others will do the same toward you.

THREE WAYS TO WRITE AND SEND EMAILS THAT ACTUALLY GET READ

Ah, emails at work—so many of them. So many. Cluttered inboxes can be overwhelming! Here are some guidelines for emailing in the workplace:

1. **Try not to send too many;** reserve emailing for important things (and yes, that's subjective!). Have a question? Go ask the person . . . in person! Keep emails professional and to the point. Don't send long emails and *please* don't hit "reply all" in a group email! We all hate that!

2. **Keep emails respectful and professional and avoid typos.** Emails may be informal, or they may have some degree of formality to them, but always be professional. Consider writing your email out in its entirety and then copying into your email program to send, to avoid the dreaded accidental send when you're only halfway done.

3. **Your work email address is for work only.** Unless there's a genuine emergency, don't use it for anything personal. Sometimes, people share funny or inspirational stories via office email, but there are endless stories of inappropriate and/or offensive material being shared. And it usually doesn't end well for the sender.

One final note:

Increasing numbers of companies now monitor their employees' email and internet use, and if you are found to be sending out things you shouldn't be, even if they wouldn't be considered offensive, you could end up in a lot of trouble. Reprimands and even firings are common, and the law tends to side with companies on this. Keep your topics professional and related to work, and you'll be just fine.

> "Whatever you can say in a meeting, you can put in an email. If I have questions, I'll tell you via email."
>
> —MARK CUBAN

SEVEN TIPS FOR GREAT PHONE ETIQUETTE

We rely so much on our phones these days that we sometimes forget that they are actually . . . phones, especially since they are so good for taking selfies and watching cat videos. But many workplaces still rely on the old-fashioned landline for communications, and since we can't text with them, we have no choice but to pick them up and talk to other human beings, a thought that can leave many people's stomachs in knots. In those situations where you'll be talking with others about business-related topics, here are some general guidelines.

1. **Office phones are for work subjects only,** unless there is a genuine emergency.

2. **Talk on phones the traditional way (i.e., holding the phone to your ear and mouth).** Don't use the speaker-phone setting, unless it is a phone meeting, or you're in a private room; you don't want to be annoying everyone else in the office! If you are using a speaker phone, let the person on the other end know. Sometimes these can distort sound and be difficult to hear. The same goes for using a headset.

3. **Speak clearly and be sure that you can hear each other.** Keep on topic, be prepared, and don't waste the other person's time.

4. **Be polite and wait your turn.** Don't interrupt or talk over the other person.

5. **You must conduct yourself with courtesy and professionalism at all times.** Some conversations may be tense, or maybe you just don't like the person you're speaking with; that doesn't matter. You're representing your company, so do it well.

6. **Thank the person at the end of the call,** and if further conversations are necessary, discuss how those will be set up.

7. **Your personal cell phone should not be used, unless that's your company's policy,** or your business is intimately tied to your phone. In that case, all the same advice applies. It may be that some texting or other communications are allowed but be sure to follow company guidelines at all times—no exceptions. Anything you say on a work phone could potentially be used against you in the future.

Phone conversations can make some people queasy at the thought of them, but if you stick to these guidelines, you'll see that the experience flows well, and you may just find yourself looking forward to this relatively old-fashioned way of communicating!

TEN TIPS FOR GOOD SLACK ETIQUETTE

If your company isn't using Slack, you've probably heard of it. It's a virtual communication platform that allows direct messaging, groups, chat rooms, file management, and various other features. Teams use it to stay in touch, bounce ideas back and forth, and keep focused. But, like any messaging or email program, there are rules for good conduct. If you're new to Slack, or already use it, here are some important short tips to keep in mind.

1. **Use Slack for work-related matters only.** Though you probably know everyone on it, don't clutter it up with personal photos and unnecessary communication. As always, keep your work and private life separate.

2. **Use public channels for much of your communication.** Since this is a work program, most of your conversations will likely be work-related, so it makes sense to share information around. If something needs to be said privately, then by all means use a DM, but remember that if you need a quicker response, a public channel will probably get it to you.

3. **Watch your tone on public channels.** Remember, this is a work tool, so be careful about being overly jokey or vulgar. Read through other messages and get a sense of how you should respond and what you should say. Use threads to keep conversations going and keep the channel manageable.

4. **Don't add someone to the public channel without DMing them first.** Remember how annoyed you were when someone added you to a social media group without asking you? Yeah, it's like that. Don't do it.

5. **Try to be prompt in responding, and if you need to leave a channel discussion, let others know.** If you just disappear mysteriously, people will wonder what happened.

6. **Push notifying (tagging someone with the @ sign) can seem a bit rude, so don't do it unless it's urgent:** "@John will do that on Friday." John may well not need to be notified about this.

7. **Emojis rule on Slack, so use them.** They're great for quick follow-ups and for highlighting important points in longer messages. Take the time to familiarize yourself with what various emojis mean in context. Be careful about overuse or inappropriate use, though.

8. **If you are sending a DM, put your whole message in it.** This reduces the number of notifications. You don't like getting constant notifications, so don't do it to someone else.

9. **Leave Slack at the office.** It's not just another social app, so let it be for work only. Use the Do Not Disturb function for after-hours and encourage everyone else to do the same.

10. **Be mindful of all the usual aspects of office etiquette.** Be polite and respectful of others' time and personal space, don't harass or argue, and remember, your boss can probably see everything you post.

SIX ESSENTIAL SOCIAL MEDIA DOS AND DON'TS

Whether you see it as a blessing or a curse, no one can escape the presence of social media. People checking their phone, laptops, and myriad devices has become so much a part of the landscape that we don't even notice them anymore. And while this may be acceptable on your own time, you'll have to modify your behavior. Here are some dos and don'ts for workplace social media use.

1. **Your personal profiles are just that: personal. Don't spend time accessing them at work.**

Many companies now have policies about this in place, and you'll need to be sure to read up on what you can and cannot do. Do not create any new personal social media accounts using your workplace email.

2. **Do not use your personal profile to criticize your company or your coworkers, or to discuss any sensitive work matters, even on your own time.** If you have access to proprietary information, don't share any of it online, ever. Any of these actions could land you in legal trouble, or get you fired.

3. **Refrain from gossip and rumors at all times,** which can spread like wildfires through re-shares. Refrain from it at all times, and don't share those embarrassing office party photos!

4. Don't criticize your company's competitors. While you may think you're showing support for your own company, it just makes you look petty and unprofessional and reflects badly on your employer.

5. Company-based social media accounts are meant for work-related subjects only, and all of the advice given above also applies.

6. With this in mind, you do have rights: No employer or potential employer can request access to your personal social media accounts (wanting passwords or asking you to log in while in their presence, for example). If an interviewer requests this information, they are breaking the law and may be guilty of discrimination or attempting to use what they find to disqualify you. Do not share this information, but instead report them (see Resources, page 164).

Confine your personal social media activity to your own time and you'll avoid a potential minefield of complications.

HOW TO ACE WORKPLACE INTRODUCTIONS

Introductions can be straightforward and easy, or they can cause all kinds of problems. If you're working at a small company, remembering everyone might be a breeze, but there's a good chance you'll be working at a much larger company, which can have multiple departments filled with people, supervisors, and more names than you think you'll ever be able to keep track of. Once established at a company, you may also have to lead introductions to visitors and outsiders. These tips will help you navigate the ocean of names and introduction etiquette a little more easily.

• **If you are new, it's fine to ask your boss to introduce you to others in the office on your first day.** In fact, they may well offer to do so. As you go around meeting new people, a good way to remember them is to shake their hands and repeat their names back to them: "Mary, I'm George, nice to meet you!" This verbalization helps cement the name in your mind. You might also want to send your main coworkers a follow-up email, using their name and saying again that you enjoyed meeting them.

• **It is also perfectly acceptable for you to take the initiative and introduce yourself to others,** if you feel comfortable doing so. A greeting followed by identifying your position will be just fine.

- **If your company is large enough to have an organization chart, ask for a copy.** It will give you a good sense of who's who and who does what.

- **Always try to remember how the person wants to be addressed.** If someone's full name is Benjamin, but he prefers "Ben," honor that wish.

- **Remember that you will likely forget some people's names, so don't feel like a failure during your first week!** Also, others will probably forget your name, too, so don't be offended. A simple, "sorry, I've forgotten your name" is an easy remedy. Please don't waste time trying to guess others' names!

- **When making introductions within the company, or for guests, some simple rules apply:** Introduce junior employees to senior ones ("Mark, this is Janet, who is in charge of Accounting"). Introduce outsiders to company people ("Susan, this is my supervisor, Tom. Tom, Susan is from our branch office in Sacramento"), whether they are business colleagues or customers.

Some people are "name people," and some people are "face people." But remembering names need not be stressful, and as you will see in the next section, with a little practice, you'll probably find that you won't have trouble keeping track of who's who.

TRICKS FOR REMEMBERING EVERYONE'S NAME —THE FIRST TIME

In the process of meeting new people, you will be called on to remember names, often a lot of them. This need not be stressful, and as mentioned, you will forget sometimes, but here are some techniques you can use to help you retain names better, so you don't have to feel embarrassed that you recognize someone's face, but not their name.

- **Focus on who you are meeting in that moment,** giving them your full attention.

- **Say their name back to them as you greet them,** and shake their hand.

- **Try to use their name again during the conversation,** if you are conversing with them after the first introduction even if it's when wrapping up: "OK, Jen, it was great to meet you!"

- **Focus on something distinguishing about them:** a facial feature, hairstyle, etc., that you can associate with their name. Association is one of the key ways that we remember.

- **Try to create an image that you can associate with the name.** Making a mental picture of it will go a long way toward cementing it in your mind. Their name may sound like something else: "Paul" sounds a bit like "ball." "Mike" might remind you of "microphone." Be creative here and see what works for you. Again, association will help you recall later.

- **Link the name to something you are already familiar with.** If the person has the same first name as your favorite musician or actor, for example, that might be a way of creating a lasting impression.

- **If you are in a social situation (such as an office party), try to introduce them to someone else soon after.** Using their name again and saying it out loud will help you match it with their face.

- **More complex names or names from an unfamiliar culture may prove to be more challenging.** It is entirely acceptable to ask someone about it, to spell it for you, even to write it down. If it's appropriate, ask for their email address, as well. You're communicating that they are important to you and that you want to know that information and remember it in the future. If someone took the time to ask you to write down your name and contact information for them, you'd feel like you were important, and that you'd made a meaningful connection. Don't be afraid to do that for someone else.

Again, don't stress too much about it! You can always ask again. Not everyone will remember who you are either and it can even be a fun way to bond with someone: "I'm so terrible with names! One time I even forgot my dad's first name when I . . . " And then you're off into a story that's a conversation starter and maybe will get a laugh or two. We're all human and everyone forgets. But using these simple techniques, with a little practice, will probably help you retain more names more often.

HOW TO COPE WITH MEETINGS

Everyone hates meetings. Well, maybe not everyone, but they do seem to be the one topic that everyone at a workplace likes to complain about. Too many meetings, meetings that are too long, meeting about meetings . . . they do have a way of bringing people together to complain about them! Unfortunately, in-person meetings are a part of office life (some estimates say that they take up about twelve hours out of any given work week), and you will get roped into attending them whether you want to or not. Here is a handy survival guide to being a stellar meeting attendee:

- **Some meetings will be productive, interesting, and helpful. And some will not.** No matter what kind of meeting it is, show up on time (or even a few minutes early), be prepared, and be attentive.

- **It's fine to ask for the details or an agenda for the meeting beforehand** (it may well be sent out to all attendees). If you need to bring materials or information with you, be sure to do so.

- **During the meeting, be attentive to others when they are speaking.** Don't interrupt or be rude in any way. If you have questions, or a counter point to make, wait until it is your turn to speak, or there is an

appropriate moment to do so. When that time comes, don't hesitate to ask questions and receive clarification.

- **Things may sometimes meander off-topic, and that might be a good thing or a bad thing.** If it's a bad thing, it's OK to gently direct everyone's attention back to the subject at hand, as long as you remain polite about it.

- **Turn off your phone** and don't try to secretly check your messages, tempting though it might be!

- **The meeting might be dull. Or pointless. Or a waste of your time better spent on something else.** It will happen, but you don't really have much of a choice but to slog through it. If these kinds of meetings are getting too regular, it may be worth sitting down with your boss or supervisor and letting them know about your concerns, especially if you have ideas for how meetings could be improved or streamlined.

- **Sometimes, you may not able to attend a meeting you are supposed to attend.** It should be for a legitimate reason, since there are only so many sick relatives you can have! It's fine to bow out if you have to, but be sure to let the organizer and your colleagues know, so that they can fill you in on the details later. You might be missing important information that you'll need later on. Really.

Office meetings are a part of office life, but you can make the most of them by being prepared, being attentive, and keeping the discussion on track.

TEN TIPS FOR ORGANIZING MEETINGS

At some point, it may be your turn to lead a meeting (gulp!). Whether you are an employee or are in a supervisor's position, how can you ensure that it doesn't turn into the kind of runaway mess or crashing bore that you hate? One simple way is to make sure you structure it so that it doesn't do any of the things that you and everyone else dislike so much!

1. **You might call a meeting for numerous reasons:** team collaboration, sharing information, progress reports for an ongoing project, brainstorming sessions, fixing problems, offering new training, orientations for new employees, and so on. Your unique workplace environment will determine the subject and how often meetings need to take place.

2. **Make your objectives and agenda clear to everyone attending before the meeting starts.** That will give them the best chance to be prepared.

3. **Remember that everyone is giving up their time to be there, so respect that and structure your meetings accordingly.** It's usually a good idea to keep meetings to thirty minutes or less, unless there is something very important that needs extra attention. Allot a specific amount of time to each subject you need to go over and try to keep it within that time frame.

4. **However, make sure there is also time for meeting attendees to have some input.** Don't cram your agenda so full that there is no room for feedback.

5. **Only ask those to attend who really need to be there.** Bringing in extra people who are not relevant to the matter at hand just wastes their time.

6. **Go in with a positive attitude and try to keep things interesting.** There are many possibilities, depending on the nature of the meeting: include videos, invite round-table discussions, have a guest speaker, or try meeting off-site somewhere. Use your imagination!

7. **Again, keep the meeting on topic(s), and if it starts to veer too far off in another direction, gently bring it back.** Remind attendees of the main purpose of the meeting, if necessary, and that you only have the room for a certain amount of time.

8. **If someone is late,** it is their responsibility to catch up.

9. **End your meeting with a "where we go from here" closer.** Meetings should set up what's to come, but not necessarily more meetings!

10. **Don't call for any more meetings than you absolutely need to.** Given what a bad reputation they often have, the fewer you can organize, the better!

Meetings can be very useful tools, and yes, they are sometimes even necessary. Keeping on point and only using them when needed will ensure that you get the most out of them, and your coworkers and employees will appreciate your approach!

HOW TO PARTICIPATE
IN VIDEO CONFERENCES

Videoconferencing has grown greatly in popularity in recent years, as technology allows people to have meetings and conversations with their colleagues literally all over the world. As long as time zones are respected, you can now have face-to-face meetings with associates in London, Tokyo, or anywhere, as individuals or in groups. This opens up countless new possibilities for collaboration and the bouncing around of ideas, but just as with meetings, there are certain protocols and ways of acting that need to be observed. Here are some top tips to make the most of your conferences. If you are having a meeting with an overseas colleague, you might want to also check out the international etiquette advice in chapter 5.

- **Be on time.** This is especially important if you are meeting across time zones. Even an hour difference can cause confusion, so make sure you know exactly when the meeting will start in your own time zone.

- **Test your equipment and setup before the meeting.** If anything goes wrong, you may not be able to fix it while the meeting is underway, and this will reflect badly on you and your company. Make sure you have everything you need, especially if you are joining a larger group for the conference. You don't want to be left out!

- **Make sure you are framed properly by your camera.** If they can only see you from the mouth down, or the left side of your face, you're going to look pretty silly, which is not the impression you want to make. Get it right before the call begins. Also, be sure you are lit properly, not too darkly, not too brightly.

- **Use a dedicated headset and microphone.** Laptop microphones and speakers are often not adequate and can send a lot of background noise to the other parties. You don't want to be seen leaning in to your laptop struggling to hear what someone else is saying.

- **Dress appropriately, even if you're at home.** You'll be seen by others and you want to present yourself accordingly. Keep your immediate surroundings clean and tidy as well, because everyone is going to see them.

- **Mute yourself when you are not speaking.** Even if you are alone, this will remove excess background noise.

- **Unmute yourself when you are speaking.** Conversely, don't give your masterful pitch only to find out that no one could hear you!

- **Give the video meeting your full attention.** Just as with an in-person meeting, don't check your email, text, or do anything else while the video conference is going on; it's just rude. Everyone participating deserves your full attention, just as you will expect it from them when it's your turn to speak.

NETWORKING LIKE A PRO

Networking conjures up all sorts of images about making important contacts and using what you've learned and who you've met to help yourself get ahead, but in reality, networking should always be mutually beneficial. It's not just about giving yourself advantages; it's seeing what you can bring to others. True networking is not even necessarily about helping you advance from your current position to something better; it can and should be about helping you be better at your current job. Here are some useful tips:

- **When networking, keep the golden rule in mind:** offer your help to others in the way that you'd want them to offer theirs to you. Raise each other up.

- **Networking is not about seeking favors or a step up;** it's about building new relationships that can have more impact in the long run than any quick fix you might be looking for. Maintaining friendships with others over time is always a better way to go, for you as well as them.

- **Identify your reasons for networking:** job advancement, meeting potential new colleagues, seeking assistance, improving your skills or learning new ones, offering your expertise or mentorship. All of these and more may be why you want to connect with others.

- **Make a list of the things you can offer:** subject knowledge, expertise, advice, and more. Be willing to give these things without the expectation of getting anything back at first. You may well find that you will be called on to assist someone or some department in some way, and that help will not be forgotten.

- **Build contact lists based on your interests and goals,** as well as what you can offer specific people or groups in return. These may be within your company itself, or outside of it within the larger industry. Within your workplace, introducing yourself in person is great if you can. Outside of it, a friendly email might be the best way to begin a conversation, with a follow-up phone call if it seems appropriate.

- **After the introduction, it might be worth the time for both of you to meet.** This might be a quick exchange, a more formal work project, or even something a bit more casual, such as lunch or coffee. Think of these experiences as expanding your social circle and making new friends, because that's really what you're doing.

Using these techniques will allow you to gradually build your social circle and introduce you to new people and potential new opportunities. It won't happen overnight; this is all about a gradual building up of networks, contacts, and new friends. But establishing new contacts and making friends will more than pay you back for the time you invest in it now.

INSIDER BUSINESS-SPEAK AND JARGON (THAT YOU'LL PROBABLY ENCOUNTER)

> Business-speak and business jargon are, unfortunately, all too common. Annoying buzzwords seem to come and go, with the workplace seeing some of the worst of them. While it's not necessary to hop on the jargon train and use them yourself (in fact, please don't!), here is a quick reference to some of the more common words you might encounter. Some of them you probably already know, some of them are mildly useful, and some of them will probably just make you cringe.

ask: This is a verb but has become a noun: "I have an 'ask' about this." No, you don't. You have a question.

best practice: A preferred method that offers the finest results. Because who would want someone's worst practice?

bio break: A bathroom break. Seriously.

bleeding edge: Even more cutting-edge than cutting edge!

blue sky thinking: Creative thinking where the sky's the limit. At least this one sort of makes sense!

boil the ocean: This means to waste time. Just like using this phrase.

burning platform: Something is in trouble. This one kind of makes sense.

dogfooding: When a company uses its own product. Theoretically quality control, but does this word *really* communicate that?!

drill down: To investigate something in more detail.

full service: A favorite of companies that like to advertise that they provide everything for their clients. Unless that "everything" includes filling up their gas tanks and shopping for their groceries, it's probably not true.

gain traction: To gain popularity. This one has been around for a while outside of the business world, but it's still there.

impact: A noun now used as a verb. Try to avoid being impacted by it.

it is what it is: Indeed, it is.

learning: One of the more egregious recent examples, a "learning" is a verb made into a noun: "I had a learning from this experience." How is this easier than just saying "I learned something"?

let's talk that: It means exactly what you think it does, but it's still silly.

leverage: One of the oldest bits of jargon, here the word is a verb for how to manipulate a situation to one's advantage. Only this sounds nicer.

low-hanging fruit: Something easy to do or accomplish with a quick fix (i.e., easy to pick off the proverbial tree). Or you could simply say it's easy.

move the needle: Get a reaction. Like an earthquake. Or something.

net-new: New, now in two words instead of one, that's new!

open the kimono: To reveal secrets or new information. It's also more than a bit racist, sexist, and just plain creepy.

out of pocket: It used to mean paying for something yourself, but now it means to be unavailable. For some reason.

 price point: The price of something, but instead of using one word, you use two.

ramp-up: An increase in production in anticipation of an increase in demand. Because things go up ramps, or something.

scalable: Another massively overused buzzword, it refers to a business or product that requires work up-front, but less effort or cost to maintain once it's actually up and running.

solution: An overused bit of jargon that seems to mean pretty much anything these days.

SWAT team: A group of "experts" brought in to solve a problem. See *tiger team*, which is even sillier.

synergize: To collaborate and/or cooperate. That's it. That's all.

to take offline: This doesn't usually have anything to do with the internet; it refers to putting a problem or issue on the back burner until later.

thought shower: Brainstorming, but "taking a shower" in thoughts. Showers, storms, it's all about what falls on you, apparently. Sometimes called an "idea shower," which is no better.

tiger team: A group of experts put together to fix a problem. One that hopefully doesn't involve raw meat and tranquilizers. See *SWAT team*, which is no better as a term.

vertical: An area of expertise. "We're consultants for the financial vertical." So what does that make a horizontal, then?

wordsmith: To revise, to rewrite. "This document needs some wordsmithing." Get out the hammer and anvil!

HOW TO BE AMAZING AT TIME MANAGEMENT

Time is something all of us never seem to have enough of. Even when we think we're on top of things, we can find ourselves with not nearly enough time to complete a task or project, or perhaps we're taking work home because it's not finished, which cuts into our important (and even necessary) personal time. Here are some tips on how to make sure you manage your time, rather than the other way around.

- **Get in the habit of prioritizing.** Start each day by focusing on the most important or urgent tasks, leaving the others, which likely can carry over to the next day. Also, be sure to rank the important tasks by those that need attention sooner.

- **Set a schedule for yourself and stick to it.** It doesn't have to be exceptionally rigid, but it should be detailed enough that you know pretty much what you will be doing for the day.

- **Creating a daily to-do list can be a great help in seeing everything you have on your plate.** If you keep it all in your head, it will be more difficult to grasp the scope, and you'll likely forget things. Write it down!

- **Make deadlines and stick to them.** If you have important tasks, know when they are due, and make sure they are completed on time, before anything else gets in their way. If you have a bit more control over when a project or task needs to be completed, it's still important to create your own deadlines and try to abide by them. This will help with prioritizing.

- **Multitasking can frequently be your enemy,** as it's easy to get distracted. If possible, try to only work on one task or project at a time, and tick them off as you finish them.

- **Be careful about taking on too much,** and if your work seems to be overwhelming, talk with your boss about it.

- **Set boundaries for yourself, and don't allow outside distractions.** Obviously, things will come up that need your attention, but for less urgent matters, try to deflect and put them off until you've accomplished what you need to do. Yes, this also means disciplining yourself to stay off the internet and your phone until break time.

- **If it's appropriate, consider delegating some of your work to a colleague who can help.** If a coworker has a bit of time to help you on a big task, then make use of that. Remember that this should be reciprocal; if you find yourself with unexpected free time, reach out and see if any of your coworkers need assistance.

- **Having said that, it's important to realize that you can't be a work machine,** who sits at a desk all day, and does nothing else; our brains don't do well in that state. Block out a little time every hour or two to get up, walk around, stretch, have a cup of coffee, check your phone for two minutes. Even a quick break from the task at hand can

leave you feeling refreshed enough to come back to it in a better state of mind. Knowing that you have a small reward every, say, ninety minutes can also keep you focused.

- **There are a number of apps and programs that can help you with scheduling, time management, and similar things.** Investigate if one or more of these might be right for you.

- **Procrastination is your enemy.** Look into ways of avoiding it and remember it's always better to do it today if it can be done and needs to be done.

[
"Procrastination makes easy things hard, hard things harder."

—MASON COOLEY
]

SURVIVING AND THRIVING IN AN OPEN OFFICE ENVIRONMENT

It used to be common that everyone at a workplace had their own space, usually a cubicle of some sort. While this is still true in many companies, it's also not uncommon for some employers to throw everyone together in an "open office," which involves people setting up and working at tables in full view of everyone else. In theory, the idea (in addition to saving money) is to encourage collaboration and team-building. In practice, a lot of people don't like it; studies have shown that productivity in open offices can indeed go down. There is some movement away from this model and toward "flexible spaces" that offer a variety of environments for different kinds of employees.

Related to this is the idea of "hot-desking," which is basically having no assigned work area in an open space and just selecting one on a first-come, first-served basis (i.e., the people that get there at 8:00 a.m. get the good seats!). This may seem like a good idea, but it has caused a number of problems. If everyone is sitting in different places every day, it's hard to find the people you need, ask questions, have quick meetings, and any number of other annoyances. Sometimes teams of people are assigned an area, but the seating is up for grabs. It all seems kind of confusing and counterproductive, but some companies do embrace it.

If you're easily distracted, introverted, work better on your own, or any number of other reasons, you could find being in an open office challenging. Or maybe you flourish in this kind of environment. Here are some tips on how to make the most of it, or at least not let it get to you.

- **Remember that you're all there to work.** While collaboration is encouraged, let others do their own work when they need to. Constant interruptions slow down the project. Conversely, this respect applies to you, too. You don't have to put up with those same constant interruptions. If you're in the middle of something and don't want to be disturbed, politely remind your coworkers that you're working and will get back to them when you can. You deserve the same privacy you give to others! On that note…

- **Keep distractions to a minimum, and don't distract others.** If you can work listening to music, then put in the earbuds and do it. This will also help you tune out noise and focus on your own work. It gives you a bit of privacy in an open space.

- **Keep your area clean, and expect that of your coworkers, too.** Also, don't let your work and materials spill over into someone else's space and don't intrude by taking it over.

- **Be mindful of strong food smells.** Your burger topped with onions and extra melted Limburger cheese may be delicious to you, but your colleagues probably don't want to have its pungent aromas drifting their way. Eat in the break room or go outside. The same goes for personal scents and perfumes. Make sure that whatever you wear isn't noticeable from more than a foot or two away. Remember that some people can have strong allergic reactions to scents, and your company may have a policy about not wearing them at work. Check first and when in doubt, don't. It should go without saying that this courtesy also applies to bathing regularly and keeping yourself clean. Please do!

- **If you get sick, stay home!** Yes, this one can be difficult, especially if you're working on a project with a deadline, but remember that in an open space, you're much more likely to infect others if you show up with a raging head cold, or the flu, or bubonic plague, or whatever. If you're really needed, see if you can arrange to do some work from home, assuming you're up to it. At the very least, try to sit far away from others and keep your area clean.

- **Just remember to be respectful of others and expect the same from them.** The golden rule applies here. Treat others with respect and expect the same in return. If issues arise (and they will), try to talk through them, using the conflict resolution ideas in chapter 4. You may also need to include your boss on any issues.

> **"I don't have an office. I sit in a cubicle with everyone else. That's partly so no one can ask for an office, which in a fast-growing company isn't practical. But it's also so I can keep my finger on the pulse of how people are feeling."**
>
> **—KEVIN P. RYAN**

BREAK ROOM ETIQUETTE, OR, NEVER LEAVE THE COFFEE MAKER EMPTY

The break room is a place of coffee, and refuge . . . and coffee. Just about every company has one, and you'll make friends with it in a hurry. It is a shared space with every other employee, so it should be obvious that you have to conduct yourself in a decent and respectful manner while using it, and even after leaving. Here are some important points to keep in mind while downing your sandwich.

- **Keep it clean!** This should be a no-brainer, but nobody wants to come in and see wrappers, containers, and food bits staining the tables or counters. Clean up after yourself, and ask others to do the same. Wash any dishes and silverware you use, and wipe down the counters or table. Bigger jobs, like cleaning the microwave or the refrigerator should be allocated out on a rotating schedule. Everyone should have the pleasure of chipping in to keep communal appliances clean, after all!

- **If you drink the last of the coffee, brew more before leaving.** It's coffee. It's necessary for life. Don't let your fellow employees down. If your workplace has a coffee pod machine, so much the better! Just make sure that it's kept clean and supplies are on hand.

- **Don't mooch other people's food, unless it is specifically**

labeled as being for everyone! Goodness, this should be obvious, but it's one of the number one complaints about break room etiquette breaches. Put simply, don't take food that doesn't belong to you!

• **Label your own food.** In addition to marking out what you brought as yours, it can also prevent mix-ups where someone accidentally grabs your salad or sandwich by mistake. Also, if it does get taken when it has your name on it, you'll know it's much more likely that someone took it on purpose…

• **Be mindful of what you put in the microwave.** Some foods, like fish, can be, well, pungent. Your colleagues back at their cubicles might not appreciate the aroma of your leftover garlic-seasoned trout wafting through their airspace. Use common sense and don't inflict certain foods on everyone else.

• **Don't leave stinky food in the refrigerator,** and don't use the fridge to store food for days. You know what happens when some foods get shoved to the back of your own fridge: new life-forms begin to mutate, multiply, and gain sentience. And come on, nobody wants to see (or smell) your moldy half-eaten falafel wrap from last week.

• **Let the break room actually be a break room.** Don't bring your work, or problems, or gossip to the room from your desk or cubicle. Give yourself a few minutes to get away from it all, and allow others the same courtesy. If someone insists on lugging their daily baggage in with them, maybe consider having a quick talk with them, or posting a sign requesting that everyone refrain from talking about work topics. Also, try not to let conversations get too loud or animated, as this can disturb those who are working closer to the break room than you might be. Consider asking your boss to solicit opinions from everyone about how to best use the space.

The break room is crucial to your well-being and hunger satisfaction, and of course, coffee consumption. Follow these few simple tips to make its use enjoyable for everyone. The coffee must flow . . .

CHAPTER 2

HIRED, QUITTING, AND FINANCES

These are three of the most important topics you'll encounter in your job search and work life. From crafting the perfect resume and acing the interview to making sure you are compensated fairly, to knowing when it's time to move on, your career, success, and contentment will depend very much on getting these three things right. This chapter will give you the information you need to get started in navigating all three successfully.

THE PERFECT RESUME

Resumes are still essential in the job market, and how you present yours can make or break your chances of getting hired. How much information is enough? How much is too much? If resume writing terrifies you, read on. A majority of job seekers admit that they struggle with this aspect of the search. Here are some tips to get you started (Note: The exact order of these listings sometimes varies depending on the template that you use, but all of them are necessary):

• **An online profile (such as at LinkedIn) is useful to have, but it is not a substitute for a classic resume.** Have both.

• **A resume is a summary of your career and work experience, so keep the format short and simple.** Use an easy-to-read font in twelve-point, with headings for sections in fourteen-point. Don't start from scratch; look online for resume templates and builders and find one that appeals to you. Seriously, this will save you a lot of time.

• **Include all contact information at the top** (including address, phone number, websites, blogs, LinkedIn, etc.).

• **List your work experience, starting with your most recent job and going in reverse chronological order.** Briefly describe your duties at each.

• **Follow this with a list of your relevant work skills.** Software knowledge, hardware experience, whatever you can bring to the job. Try to tailor this section to specific job requirements, if you have different sets of skills.

- **List your education, again with the most recent institution first.** If you graduated with honors or awards, now is the time to brag about it!

- **List other skills,** professional affiliations, outside work (volunteer work, for example), and interests.

- **If possible, keep this all to one page.** Yes, that may seem like a tall order, especially if you have significant experience. It's acceptable to have the information carry on to a second page, but it should be no longer than that. Some employers specifically request that you keep your resume to one page, so you may have to squeeze it in. Using a font in eleven-point can help.

- **Write and rewrite this as often as you need to get it the way you want it.** You will also probably need to tailor a bit of the content to the specific wants of potential employers, so keep a master document on file and then make copies to alter as needed.

- **Look online for examples of good resumes** (there are endless sites that show these!), and feel free to borrow the formats and ideas that seem good for you.

- **Keep a digital copy** of your resume on your website or elsewhere in PDF format, so that you'll always have a clean, uncorrupted version. Update it frequently.

A resume is an essential tool in the job search, and with a little work and practice, you'll be crafting professional, easy-to-read, and impressive examples that will put you in the best light for employers.

ALL ABOUT YOUR ONLINE PROFILE

For purposes of this book, "online profile" means professional sites, such as those at LinkedIn and related sites. Instagram, Twitter, Facebook, and all the rest aren't relevant here (though your company may well have pages on those sites). Professional social media sites offer a great chance to expand on your resume, make valuable connections, find a new job, network, and makes things easier and more interesting. Don't hesitate to dive into using this valuable online tool! Your LinkedIn or other profiles, however, should be created with the intention of being seen by employers and coworkers. Here is how to optimize yours.

- **Take the time to complete your profile.** A half-finished one doesn't transmit that you're serious about reaching out to others.

- **Include a photo of yourself.** This may seem obvious, but it makes a difference. Putting a face to a name is always better when people are searching. It is worth investing in a professional headshot, rather than using a phone selfie, since this is the first that others will see of you.

- **If you can customize and personalize the URL to your page, do so.** JaneDoe.com looks much better than Webhost.com/JaneDoe. It's well worth investing in a URL for your own site.

- **If you can customize your profile with a cover photo or similar options, do so.** It will make you stand out. Just make sure that the image is appropriate for what you want to convey.

- **If you can add a personalized, catchy headline, do it!** This may be the first thing that someone sees, along with your photo.

- **Take the time to craft an interesting summary that plays to your strengths and keeps your target audience in mind.** There are several guides online that will help you. It should be a few paragraphs long, but not so lengthy that others tune out when reading it. Write in first person; writing in third person sounds pompous and can be off-putting. Try to be warm and inviting, not formal.

- **Avoid using jargon words** (see chapter 1, pages 38–41, for a list of some common offenders).

- **Treat your profile as a chance to craft an extended resume or CV,** but with a more conversational tone.

- **With LinkedIn, be sure to include a current job or title entry,** because this is what recruiters and hiring agents will most often look for. If you are unemployed, simply list what you want to be doing, and define it as "seeking new opportunity" or something similar.

- **The more you can stand out, the better.** Many of these kinds of sites support multimedia, so if you have relevant photos, videos, blogs, or other media, be sure to include them.

- **Recommendations and endorsements can be great social proof,** but you are not obligated to include every one of them. Be choosy about what you display, to show yourself at your best.

- **Keep you profile updated regularly.** Any time you have something relevant to add (a new skill, a completed team project, a successful launch.), be sure to add it.

- **Try to get connected with more than fifty people,** but don't just go around randomly collecting strangers. Connect with people who are relevant to you, your field, and your interests.

- **Most of these sites have privacy settings.** If you are currently employed but are seeking a new job via LinkedIn, keep it hidden from your coworkers using privacy settings. If news of it gets back to your employer, things could get awkward.

- **Keep your professional profile separate from your personal ones** and tailor your content accordingly.

It's important to remember that your employer or potential employer is not legally allowed to ask you for passwords and/or access to your personal social media sites. However, there is nothing to prevent them from browsing what you post publicly. If you have some concerns about that, then make your personal profiles private (viewable by friends only), and remember that if an employer offers to connect with you as "friends" to your personal pages, this is also inappropriate. They're more than likely just trying to snoop.

NAILING THE JOB INTERVIEW

There probably aren't too many things more stressful than a job interview! Some say it's as bad, if not worse, than stage fright. You can feel like everything is riding on how you do in those few minutes when some cold interviewer gives you the hard stare and is seemingly just waiting for you to make any mistake, the slightest little error, so they can stamp your resume as "rejected" and move on to someone who is clearly way more qualified.

Interviews don't have to be that nerve-racking. The fact that you have been called for one at all is a testimony to your skill and experience. Obviously, they saw *something* that they liked, so by being prepared you can give them even more to be impressed with when the time comes. Here are some ways to prepare for the big day:

- **Research the company and learn about them beforehand;** search their website and their social media for information. But this shouldn't just be about memorizing facts and figures, quarterly sales, and so forth. Instead, get a feel for the company culture, the "vibe," the dress code, any special events, casual Fridays. Show that you can fit right in to these things. Are they about to launch some new product? Have they just reached a company milestone? Read up on it and show your enthusiasm.

- **Try to learn who will be interviewing you.** In a smaller company, it might well be the boss; in a larger, it could be HR. You'll be better able to tailor your answers and approach if you know who you'll be sitting with at the interview.

- **Dress appropriately, make eye contact, and sit up straight . . .** basically all of the manners that you learned as a child are important here! Looking or acting like a slob is a surefire way to get rejected.

- **Practice what you will say well ahead of time.** Write things down and read them out, if necessary. Eventually, it will sink in and you'll feel more comfortable.

- **Breathe deeply and relax as you enter the interview room.** If you are especially worried about nerves, research some simple relaxation techniques online and try them out in the days before your interview.

- **Turn off your cell phone and leave it off.** Always.

- **Prepare a short list of the best "selling points" about yourself.** You are likely competing against others and you need to make yourself stand out.

- **Some suggest that the first five minutes of your interview is crucial, so bring positive energy and enthusiasm.** Show them that you're glad to be there and eager to work with them, both now and going forward. Be positive throughout the interview, don't go negative! Remember that the interviewer may be seeing several candidates in one go and might be tired, so make their job easy for them.

- **Have questions prepared and be ready to ask them throughout the interview.** Others may come up as you go along, but asking your own questions shows your interest.

- **Bring an extra copy of your resume to the interview.** Interviewers misplace them all the time (especially if interviewing multiple candidates); plus, being prepared and helpful is another point in your favor.

- **You may be asked "behavior questions,"** such as how you acted in a certain situation, how you handled stress, how you responded to something, and so on. Have examples of your reactions in mind; write them down and memorize them, if necessary.

- **If you're being interviewed by more than one person, make sure you give attention to each of them.** Don't just focus on one.

- **Always end the interview on a positive note.** Thank the interviewer for their time and the opportunity to speak with them.

- **Remember that certain interview questions are not appropriate, and are often illegal:** race, age, gender, sexual orientation, political views, religious beliefs, marital status, and even your children (or plans to have children). It's always to be hoped that you won't encounter this kind of behavior, but it does happen. A simple answer such as, "I don't believe that is relevant to this interview" may be enough to deflect, or you can answer with something about your commitment to working and giving your best to the company. Bear in mind that a company that asks these kinds of intrusive questions may not be where you want to work, anyway, and if they are prying now, it could be a red flag for similar behavior later on. If something seems especially inappropriate, it may be worth reporting them (see chapter 4).

- **There may be more than one interview.** Some companies have several rounds to determine the best candidate. This can feel like having to start all over again, but be encouraged! If you're asked back, it means that the company sees value in you and wants to know more. Much of the same advice applies, and this is also a chance to fine-tune your message and fix any minor mistakes you fear you might have made before.

This list is a lot of information to take in, but it's important to keep these points in mind. This is your chance to show yourself off at your best, so make the most of it!

> **"I think the single most important thing for a job interview is leave the phone in your bag and do not look at it for twenty minutes."**
>
> **—JOANNA COLES**

YOU'VE BEEN HIRED! NOW WHAT?

You got the job! Congratulations! Your efforts have paid off and the company recognizes you as a valuable asset. It's time to do the happy dance and celebrate in the way you feel most appropriate . . . within reason, if course. So, what can you expect between now and the time you start?

- **You'll almost certainly have paperwork, maybe lots of it.** Tax forms, other personal information (emergency contacts, for example), company materials to read up on, and so on. If you're in the United States, there may be health plan options to consider. All of this will need to be in place by the time you start, or shortly thereafter. If anything is unclear, contact HR, or whoever is in charge of the company's paperwork.

- **If you have any questions or concerns about the job itself, contact your new boss and communicate them.** Ask what they expect of you (what to bring, any special preparations, etc.). This will open a positive line of communication from the beginning.

- **Before you start the job, you may have to attend a new employee orientation.** These can be helpful as an introduction to the company and a way to meet new people, and they may last for one day, or several. Be sure you are on time and prepared.

- **Make sure to rest up the night before your first day.** You want to go in feeling good!

- **On your first day, arrive early.** If you are commuting and have the chance, practice the commute one morning beforehand to get a sense of how long it will take.

- **Make sure you know the dress code;** it's always better to be a bit more dressed up on your first day of orientation or work than to be underdressed! You can relax it a bit afterward, if the company style allows for it.

- **Practice some techniques for meeting people and remembering their names** (see chapter 1, pages 28–29), both at orientation and when you start. You'll make a great impression that way.

Waiting to start a new job can be an exciting and stressful time. Follow these steps to make sure that everything goes smoothly and you can start off with confidence.

> **"Starting a new job is always scary, or at least for me it's always scary. It's like the first day of school."**
>
> **—SEAN MAHER**

HOW TO SURVIVE YOUR FIRST WEEK

So, you've been hired, filled out all the forms, and sailed through orientation. It's all a done deal and you start next week! What can you expect? Here are some strategies for making that week a great one.

- **Introduce yourself as much as possible, when the time seems appropriate** (don't go interrupting meetings or conversations, obviously!). If you need to, practice what you're going to say ahead of time, and use the techniques for remembering names (see chapter 1, pages 28–29).

- **Ask, ask, and ask some more, and be sure to take notes.** The more questions you ask, the quicker you'll get up to speed. Seek out those with the information you need, and introduce yourself. This is also a great way to bond with your new coworkers.

- **In the spirit of asking, it might be worth trying to find a mentor or mentors,** those who can help you as you make the adjustment to your new space.

- **Learn the layout of your workplace**—restrooms, elevators, stairs, break room—if you haven't been shown already. It doesn't hurt to ask for a quick tour if you need it.

- **Consider asking out one of more of your coworkers for lunch,** if you feel comfortable doing so. And if you are invited to go to lunch or coffee by someone or a group of people, by all means, accept.

- **If it seems appropriate, step up and volunteer to help on projects and tasks.** Show that you're a part of the team from the get-go, which will impress your new boss and be appreciated by your new colleagues.

- **Be careful about committing to too much all at once, though.** Whether that means projects or social engagements, it's still a good idea to ease into your new environment. You might find yourself exhausted after your first few days, so be sure to take care of yourself.

- **Be careful about talking about your previous job in your new one,** especially if it was terrible and you couldn't wait to get out of it! That kind of negativity won't impress anyone, and may set you up to look like a complainer. If something from then is directly relevant to your new tasks, then of course, bring it up.

- **Check in with your boss regularly in those first five days, to see how you're doing,** if there is anything else needed of you, etc. Be sure to listen to their responses and advice. Your boss will appreciate your attention to your work and the enthusiasm you're bringing to it.

The first week can seem a bit daunting, but remember that you're going into an environment where it's highly likely that people are welcoming and want you to succeed. So help them to help you.

ASKING FOR A RAISE

At some point, you may feel that you offer more value to your company than you are receiving. So, you have to face asking for a raise. What if your boss says no? What if everyone tells you that you don't deserve it and laughs at you? All right, that second scenario is not likely, but the thought of it is an uncomfortable one. Asking for what we want is not easy, even when we feel we deserve it.

How can you prepare? Here are some suggestions:

- **In the meeting, establish your worth and value to the company,** show what you bring to the table, what your skills are, and how much you can contribute going forward.

- **Don't compare yourself to others.** You are you and you are unique. Also, salaries are considered private, so don't ask your colleagues what they make for a comparison. It looks bad. Really.

  - **However, it is acceptable to research the rates for comparable work in your industry** and use that as a guideline to determine your desired salary.

- **Don't be confrontational or get angry if you don't get exactly what you want.** Accept that there may be some room for negotiation. Also, don't make things personal. Sorry to say, your boss is probably not going to be swayed by stories of your struggles or hardships.

- **If the company's budget won't allow for salary increases, you probably don't have any other options but to wait until it does** or consider looking elsewhere. In all cases, remember to be polite, gracious, and professional.

Asking for a raise need not be as painful or terrifying as you fear it might be, and by following this advice, you will be in a better position to make your case and receive the compensation you feel you deserve.

> **"If I ask for money, all I get is advice. But if I ask for advice, I end up getting money."**
>
> **—JOHN QUELCH**

GETTING A COUNTEROFFER

There are different kinds of counteroffers. You may be applying for a job and negotiating a salary and need to counter the offer they've made you. You may be asking for a raise at your current job and they offer you less than you want. Or, you may be ready to leave your position and your employer offers you more money to stay. What to do? Money makes everyone and everything awkward, it seems, but you can navigate through these tricky waters with a bit of preparation.

- **If you are negotiating with a potential employer, remember that compensation includes more than money:** stock options, bonuses, extra time off, flexible work schedules, travel, etc., are all possible additions. These need to be considered in your overall package. If you have a genuine need to, say, work from home one day a week (a family commitment, for example), state that and why. Consider also how often pay raises are available. Could you take a little less now to receive more in a year?

- **If you are one of multiple potential hires, there may be a reason they can't give you more money at that time** (budgets and such), but they may be more flexible with other forms of compensation. See what's available to you and try to understand where they are coming from.

- **Be honest about your personal situation, but also try to be fair.** If it's really not doable, then you may have to decline to take the job. Just remember that hard-nosed negotiating is not going to impress anyone and will likely result in you being dropped from consideration.

- **If you are asking for a raise at your current job, and receive a counteroffer for less, try to see their situation.** The company budget may not allow for the amount you want at that time, but it doesn't mean it won't happen eventually. Can you live with a bit less than you wanted for a while? Can the raise come in increments, say, a certain amount now, followed more in six months? There may well be room for negotiation. Consider other forms of compensation, too.

- **What if you want to quit, but your employer makes you an offer of more money to keep you?** This is a tricky situation and you'll have to ask yourself some questions: Do you want to leave because you're not getting enough money? The problem may have just solved itself. Are you unhappy with your work environment? More money probably won't change that. Do you want to move on to another career? More money definitely won't change that. Perhaps you're moving a long distance away, or there is some other nonnegotiable on the table. In that case, thank your employer and politely decline.

- **What if you've been offered more money by another company,** and when announcing your intent to leave, your current employer matches or exceeds their salary as a counteroffer to keep you? This is tricky, and there is no easy answer. If the only reason you're leaving is for more money, it might be worth taking the counteroffer. On the other hand, if you were so valuable to begin with, why did it take the fear of you leaving to get them to put up more compensation?

- **In this last situation, you'll have to decide if you really want to stay,** or if there are other factors. Is this extra money going to come with tons of new responsibilities? Will there be resentment from your boss or your coworkers? Will you be able to advance in your career the way you want? Will the potential new job be a better fit for your own goals and well-being?

Money makes everything tricky, and even though it's the prime reason we are at a workplace, it's never easy to talk about. Asking for a raise or receiving counteroffers of more or less money will almost always require you to ask yourself some hard questions and evaluate your personal situation.

[
"So I want to make money. I think it's an OK goal to have. I always felt like I can't ask for that. But why not?"

—*MARY LAMBERT*
]

SEVEN TIPS FOR INTERVIEWING NEW JOB CANDIDATES

After you've been at a job for a while, and especially if the company is small, you may be called on to be part of a group interviewing potential new employees. Yes, you get to do to them what was done to you! Well, maybe not. Here are some tips for ensuring that you are helping your company pick the best candidate.

1. **Be on time and be ready.** Don't forget the candidate's resume and be sure to have read it and any other materials beforehand.

2. **Turn your cell phone off and leave it off.** If you have a laptop, don't check your emails. All of that can wait.

3. **Ask the questions you want to ask, but be sure to give the candidate time to answer.** Don't talk over them, interrupt, or be rude, no matter how bad your day might be going. Show them respect since they are giving you some of their time. Don't waste it.

4. **Engage with the interviewee and be conversational at the start.** This is not a pop quiz or a parole board meeting. This person is potentially joining your organization, so make them feel welcome. You want them relaxed so they can present themselves in the best light.

5. Answer the interviewee's questions to the best of your ability. If you genuinely don't know the answer to something, say so, and maybe offer to find out.

6. Be careful not to ask questions regarding a candidate's race, marital status, religion, sexual orientation, family situation, etc. (see the earlier entry, "Nailing the Job Interview" on page 58). These are potentially illegal. If an interviewee offers up such information unsolicited, try to steer the conversation away from it and back to the job at hand. Nothing else is important.

7. After the interview, thank them and tell them you will be in touch. And when you say that, actually *mean* it. No one likes to be left hanging. If your company chooses not to hire a given candidate, sending a short email relaying this information is not only the professional thing to do, it's just basic courtesy.

Hiring an employee is a big responsibility. And if you are called to assist in the process, it's something you need to take seriously and do to the best of your ability. Following this advice will ensure that you have the best chance of finding the right match.

HOW TO TENDER YOUR RESIGNATION

Leaving a job is always potentially uncomfortable. It depends entirely on the situation and whether your departure is amicable or not. Most commonly, you'll be giving notice. If for any reason, you feel you need to leave sooner (an abusive boss or coworker, a question of personal safety, or something illegal), please see chapter 4 for more resources and help.

For purposes of this section, we will assume that you are ready to move on, or perhaps are relocating, have accepted another position, etc. So how can you uncouple yourself from your current job in the best way?

- **Try to make the experience as positive and amicable as possible.** Don't bring up every little annoyance from the past three years. No one wants to feel uncomfortable, and it's good not to burn any bridges. In some industries, everyone knows everyone else, and your next employer might be friends with your soon-to-be ex-employer, so be careful not to bad-mouth anyone at your next job.

- **Always give your resignation in person, not by email, voice mail, or text.** You owe them that.

- **Thank your boss for the opportunity** and for what you learned and gained from the experience.

- **Two weeks' notice has long been the standard for leaving a job, but in some cases, you may need to give a longer notice.** If you are part of a group that is working on a big project, or they have need of your specialist skills, it may take them longer to find a replacement. In these situations, a month or longer might be more appropriate and courteous.

- **In a larger company, you may have an exit interview.** Be polite and refrain from attacking your boss or coworkers, even if you have grievances with them. Try to keep things positive and emphasize what you feel you've gained from your experiences.

- **If your departure is amicable, don't hesitate to reach out to your boss and coworkers for references,** and tell them how much you appreciated working with them.

Quitting a job can be stressful for a lot of reasons, so above all, try to make the actual process of leaving as smooth as possible.

> **"Please accept my resignation. I don't care to belong to any club that will have me as a member."**
>
> **—GROUCHO MARX**

HOW TO SURVIVE IN BETWEEN JOBS

At some point, you find yourself having left one job and waiting for another to begin. Or perhaps you've been laid off or downsized, and you're in the stressful situation of trying to find new employment. What can you do in those times to make things easier on yourself, and help with your day-to-day needs?

- **Realize that whatever the reason for your situation, almost everyone has gone through it themselves.** You are not alone. Reach out to friends and family if you have them near. Just talking about it can help lift the burden.

- **Keep watch on your budget and your finances.** Some belt-tightening may be necessary and those expensive coffees and nights out with friends might have to wait for a while.

- **Start searching for a new job as soon as possible.** Not only will this give you something to do, it gets you back out there. Be sure to reach out to your contacts, promote your skills, do everything you've done before. If you've developed a network of colleagues and business friends, now is the time to tap into that and reach out. Get back on LinkedIn and make use of it!

- **Commit time each day to your job search.** Set a schedule and stick to it. Make to-do lists and do them. Set longer goals and work to achieve them. Keeping active in this way will also help prevent inertia from setting in, which brings with it binge-watching TV shows and naps on the sofa.

- **While actively searching for a new job is important, be sure not to get caught up in the trap of applying for everything out there.** This is a waste of your time and will run you ragged. Focus on only those jobs that you want in the industries you are interested in. Consider also that this may be the ideal time to embark on a career shift, if that's what you've wanted to do. Career changes are becoming increasingly common and frequent and this may be the wake-up call you need to get on with it.

- **Is it time to consider freelancing?** It's not always easy, but increasing numbers of people are doing it out of desire and necessity. Research online and see if your particular area of interest might be worth pursuing, or if you've already done that, maybe try dipping your toe in a little to see what the response is. Reach out to relevant companies in your area of expertise and see if they hire freelancers. More and more do. It might help pay the bills while you wait for something more permanent to come along.

- **Make sure that you take some time for yourself, too.** You'll probably have some spare time now, so what will you do with it? Is there a book you've wanted to read? A place you've wanted to volunteer for a few hours a week? Don't make everything about the job search; you matter, too!

Being without a job is stressful. Remember to take care of yourself first. Then create a set plan for moving forward. Reach out to friends for support and colleagues for career help.

KEEPING A BRAG FILE

A "brag file" is pretty much exactly what you think it is: a collection of great things about you! It is much more than just a resume or CV. It is evidence of your great performance at your job or university that you can take with you in the future, for job interviews, reviews, client interviews, and other meetings. You should keep both digital and hard copies. Here are some things you will want to consider keeping in it.

- **Copies of college transcripts,** especially if you did well in your university days. Information about scholarships and other awards is nice to have, too.

- **Copies of your degree(s), professional certifications, licenses, and other educational markers.** Photocopies (for a physical file), online scans into PDF, etc. Have everything in one place.

- **Professional associations that you are a member of.** These don't need to be anything fancy, just organizations that might be relevant to your work. If you are not a member of any, consider searching online for your industry. These organizations can offer many useful benefits, including special resources, networking opportunities, education, and much more.

- **Previous work evaluations and performance reviews,** progress reports, and so on.

- **A few people who can write you recommendation letters.** Just be sure to get their permission to include them.

- **Samples of your work.** This could include almost anything: blogs, articles, screenshots of web designs, virtually anything that you've contributed to your job.

- **Are you in sales?** Did you help improve overall performance on one occasion or several? Put it in here.

- **Previous letters of recommendation,** communications that commend or thank you for your work and contributions. Basically, any written feedback from your boss is good to have.

- **LinkedIn recommendations** and other testimonials.

- **Evidence of outside activities:** Do you volunteer? Do you work with a charity or nonprofit? Do you have any hobbies?

- **Any press articles or photos** about you and your work.

- **Have you won any professional or personal awards?** List them.

- **You may want to keep several different versions of your brag file,** tailoring different versions to different industries or vocations.

You want to keep things relatively focused, and not just include everything you can think of; acing your third-grade spelling bee is, sadly, not relevant. But showing that you are well-rounded and have an active life in other areas is a good way of demonstrating your value for potential employers, reviewers, etc. The best employees are those that can bring a wealth of different experiences to the table. Just as colleges want to see that you are more than your high school grades, employers want to know who you are and if you'll be a good fit.

TACKLING YOUR RETIREMENT PLAN

You're in your twenties, so why on earth do you need to worry about retirement? The scary fact is, getting older sneaks up on us far faster than we would like. Thinking about setting money aside now is the best way to ensure that you'll have some security when the later decades come knocking at your door. Here are a few ways to make the most of it.

- **Start saving now.** This may seem like a tall order if you have expenses and student loans, but even a small amount set aside every month adds up over time. Ten percent is ideal, but anything helps.

- **Sign up for your employer's 401(k), if this is an option.** Most employers match your contribution up to a certain amount and the money is withheld from your paycheck, so you never have to worry about it. The best part is, that money is taken out before taxes, so you'll actually be taxed less on the remaining amount. It's a win-win!

- **If a 401(k) is not an option (and it's not always), consider opening a Roth IRA.** In this case, the money goes in after taxes, so you'll pay a bit more now, but when you withdraw it in retirement, it will be tax-free, an attractive option.

- **Investments such as stocks are another option,** just bear in mind that the market is always volatile, always going up or down, and your tolerance for stress and loss is something to consider. In the long run, stocks are usually a good investment, but in the meantime, you can go on some wild rides! Consider buying stocks in safer, more well-established companies. They may not make as much in the short term, but their chance for growth at a slow, steady pace is higher.

- **If you can, having an emergency fund in a high-yield savings account might be worth your time.** Again, you can put a small amount away each month and watch it grow over time. This can be useful for unexpected expenses, such as car repairs, new computers, medical bills, etc. And unlike retirement funds, you won't be penalized for withdrawing the money early.

Planning for the future might seem unnecessary right now, but it will probably be here before you know it and having some savings stashed away in long-term accounts will make the transition to retirement easier.

"Take free money. No matter how in debt you are, if your employer offers a matching contribution on a 401(k) or other retirement vehicle, you must sign up and contribute enough to get the maximum company match each year. Think of it as a bonus."

—SUZE ORMAN

HOW TO MAINTAIN GOOD BUSINESS RELATIONSHIPS

In the course of your working life, you'll meet people, probably lots of them. Some will come and go, some will only be at the edge of your awareness and interaction, but others will become long-term colleagues and even friends. Here are some strategies for helping to build and maintain good relationships with colleagues, clients, others in your industry, and anyone else who might be important to you.

- **Business relationships are often described as business-to-business (B2B) or business-to-customers (B2C).** Both are important in different ways. Which ones you develop more will depend on the nature of your company's business.

- **Networking is essential to building good relationships** (see Networking Like a Pro, pages 36–37). Follow the steps presented there to begin making strides toward cultivating successful business relationships and communication.

- **Determine who your best contacts are and try to reach out to them on a regular basis.** Just a quick check-in will tell them that you value them and their skills. For those who are less valuable to your immediate needs, or whom you are not as close to, even reaching out periodically is a courteous and professional thing to do.

- **When making contact with those in your network, offer your own help before asking for any from others.** If you are seen to be ready to assist, when the time comes, more people will be willing to assist you. Let people know that you are there for them.

- **Be yourself, be honest, and work toward building mutual respect and trust.** Others are not there to be used and discarded when no longer needed.

- **Don't go in with expectations.** Accept others for who they are, not who you want them to be. Someone who seemed like an excellent contact may turn out not to be, and that's fine.

 • **Occasional meetups for coffee, lunch, or something similar are ideal for maintaining and nurturing relationships.** Suggest them and accept invites when they come your way.

- **Always watch what you say,** even with colleagues with whom you are friendly and comfortable. You never know who's listening, and gossip travels exceptionally fast!

Business relationships, like all relationships, take time to build well, and respect and trust to keep. Make sure that you are reaching out to people and cultivating contacts for the right reasons and that will certainly benefit you and your company in the long run.

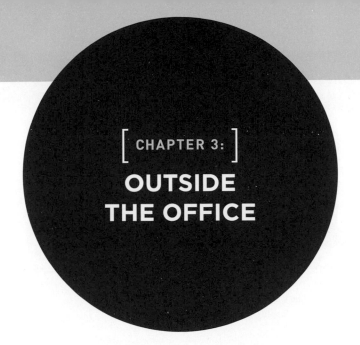

[CHAPTER 3:]

OUTSIDE
THE OFFICE

Not all of your work experiences will take place in the confines
of the office. Depending on the size and nature of your company,
you may be expected to travel for work, attend industry-related
conferences, attend business functions and award ceremonies, be
present at business dinners, and or show up for more social events
like drinks and holiday parties (and know how to separate work
colleagues from personal friends). Each of these situations can
bring its own complications and stresses, but each can also be very
rewarding both professionally and personally. This chapter offers
you a look at how to make the most out of the many out-of-office
interactions you may have, and hopefully live to tell the tale!

HOW TO NAVIGATE THE BUSINESS DINNER

The business dinner may be formal and all about company business, or it may be a social affair. If you are invited to one, what should you expect?

- **Find out how formal the venue is** and remember it's always better to overdress a little.

- **Show up on time and be ready.** Plan your travel time accordingly; arriving early is much better than being late. If you are late, call and let your colleagues know. If your host is late? Be patient and wait at least fifteen minutes before calling.

- **Greet everyone with handshakes and introductions.** Try to remember names by repeating their names back to them.

- **Wait for your host or the most senior member of the group to sit first;** in some countries this is compulsory. Sit up straight and keep your hands and elbows off the table. Learn about place settings, and learn how to use a dinner napkin (hint: do not tuck it into your shirt!).

- **Go sparingly on the alcohol; not drinking at all is fine.** If you don't drink, let them know and politely decline any offers of alcohol. If your host doesn't drink, consider not drinking yourself.

- **When ordering, wait for the more senior members of the group to order first** and take some cues from them as to what you will choose. Ordering the most expensive item on the menu is considered a bit rude. If you have any special dietary requirements, it's fine to ask the server what options the restaurant has, or call ahead and inquire.

- **If you receive your food before others, do not simply start eating;** wait until all the food has been served.

- **If you need to excuse yourself from the table, leave your napkin in your chair, not on the table.** The bathroom should really be the only reason you leave; your phone should be turned off for the duration of the dinner. If you know something personal might happen (a pregnant spouse, a loved one in the hospital), you can leave your phone on and inform your party of the situation.

- **Don't place anything on the table:** phone, napkin, purse or handbag, etc. The table is for plates, food and drink, and utensils only. Store everything else discreetly under your chair, and keep your napkin in your lap.

- **When eating, cut your food one piece at a time, rather than cutting up several pieces all at once.** Always chew with your mouth closed and don't talk at the same time. Do not blow on your food; if it's too hot, let it cool down naturally. If you are having soup, please don't slurp it and make noises! Try to eat your food at roughly the same rate as your colleagues, so that you're not sitting there with an empty plate halfway though everyone else's meal. When you have finished eating, place your knife and fork parallel to each other in the center of your plate.

- **It's assumed that your host or company will pay for the meal, unless they say otherwise.** Use your judgment and see how everyone else acts.

- **During your dinner, follow the tone of the conversation.** It may start out as a business meal and shift into something more casual, or it may be the other way around.

A business dinner can be formal or casual, stressful or enjoyable, but these basic tips should help you get the most out of it. People *do* take notice of others' behaviors. And understanding the etiquette of the evening will reflect well on you.

> **"Nothing is less important than what fork you use. Etiquette is the science of living. It embraces everything. It is ethics. It is honor."**
>
> **—EMILY POST**

GETTING THE MOST OUT OF OTHER KINDS OF BUSINESS GATHERINGS

Beyond the business dinner, there are other types of gatherings that you'll find yourself attending. This chapter discusses events such as social drinks, conferences, and holiday parties in separate sections, but here is a list of some of the other common functions that will come your way at one time or another.

- **Trade shows:** Your company may have an exhibit or booth at a local trade show in your industry, and you may be asked to staff the booth at various times during the duration of the show. This is a chance for you to put your best foot forward and represent your employer well. Be sure to read up on all materials and information about what's expected of you, your hours, etc. If it's your first time, be sure to ask for help from colleagues who have worked them before.

- **Product launches:** If your business produces items (anything from equipment to software), you will almost certainly have product launch events from time to time. These can be crucial for a company that might have spent months or even years developing the item(s) to be featured during the launch. This will be a gathering of industry leaders, probably press, the team behind the product, possibly shareholders, and others. This kind of event can be a big deal, so be sure you are prepared and know your role, if any, well in advance. If you are attending just as an

employee, be sure to be on time and show your colleagues respect; they've earned their moment in the sun!

- **Charity events**: If your company is large enough, it may choose to sponsor one or more charities or arts organizations at fundraising events. This not only helps the recipient but is excellent advertising for the company itself. These events tend to be more formal and attract those wealthy enough to make substantial donations. It's likely that such an event will be black tie, so plan on a formal evening, and as always, be on your best behavior to reflect well on the company.

- **Team-building events:** These may seem like things to make one cringe or eye roll, but they do have great value in helping group bonding, particularly for a team dedicated to a specific project. Such events may last for an afternoon, a weekend, or longer, and may be sporting events, retreats, or any combination of activities to strengthen group ties. Your participation will probably not be optional, unless you have a valid reason, such as a medical excuse, for not doing so. It's not uncommon for employers to survey their employees ahead of time, to see what they would most like to do and what they'd like to get out of such a gathering.

- **Appreciation:** Your employer may host an event to honor and reward employees who have gone beyond the call and done something excellent for the company. Or they might recognize the efforts of an entire department. These may be simple (a dinner a trip to the bar), or they may be much more lavish (a cruise, a resort break). If you or your group are the recipients, be grateful and gracious and know that your hard work is appreciated.

WHEN PRIVATE LIFE MEETS PROFESSIONAL LIFE

Obviously, you can't keep your personal and private lives completely separate. You are the same person at work and at home. But recognizing that each is a different part of you is important in maintaining good relationships at work and a healthy work-life balance. This section and the next discuss how to do that.

- **Remember that you are there to do work for your company.** Outside distractions, such as personal email, text messages, voice mail, and other personal communications are off-limits until lunch or your break. Many companies already have policies in place about this.

- **The same prohibition goes for spending time on the internet.** Unless it is job related, social media and cat videos will have to wait, to say nothing of anything more "adult-oriented." Bear in mind that your search history may be available to IT and subject to review.

- **At the very least, email and internet are distractions from why you are there,** and if you get too caught up in them, you're taking away time from your work.

- **On the other hand, studies show that most people can't concentrate on one task for more than about ninety minutes.** Know your limitations and pace yourself.

- **If extra work is being handed off to you and you feel overwhelmed,** or if you have to take it home to finish it, it is perfectly acceptable to talk with your boss or supervisor about your concerns. It may be that this is a temporary situation in the run-up to the launch of a product or initiative, and everyone has to chip in, but be aware of work and projects that are expanding, the dreaded "scope creep." You owe the company your time for your salary, but you don't owe it your entire life.

- **Find out what your company's policy on overtime is,** if you will be putting in extra hours at the office or at home in the evenings or on weekends. Asking for and expecting additional money for your extra time is completely reasonable.

- **Remember that you are not just your work.** Even if you are young, career-oriented, and don't mind putting in the extra hours to advance yourself, you need to take care of yourself. Burnout is a real thing and it can have terrible effects on your health and psychological well-being. Sometimes, you need to put yourself first.

Of course, you will never be able to fully separate your professional and personal lives, so the trick will be to find the balance between them that is right for you.

FRIENDS VERSUS COWORKERS

Your coworkers and colleagues are important. You see them daily, you work on projects together, maybe you chat at lunch or in the break room, but are they your friends? Should they be? Here are some thoughts.

- **It's important to be able to get along with your coworkers.** Friction and antagonism can make things unpleasant for everyone, but you are not obligated to form close friendships, or even much in the way of casual friendships outside of work.

- **Many experts feel that a bit of distance is healthier.** Keeping your personal and professional lives separate can benefit everyone. Research has shown that people often feel more distracted when working with close friends, because they are more invested in their personal lives and well-being.

- **This is not to say that you can't be concerned about a coworker—but remember why you are there.** Keeping a bit of emotional distance allows you to stay more focused on the tasks at hand.

- **Close friendships can lead to awkward situations.** If your best friend works with you, and they get a promotion you feel that you deserved, how is that going to affect your friendship outside of work? What if you get promoted and are now your best friend's supervisor? What if your best friend gets fired? How will that reflect on you?

- **Groups of friends tend to form cliques.** If three or four of you only ever hang out with each other at work, it may make you look standoffish to others and may impact how you work with everyone else. If you saw a small group of people constantly ignoring you and everyone else at work to be together, how would you feel about having to work on a project with them?

- **Think of being friendly instead of being friends.** It's perfectly fine to go out for coffee or lunch with different people at your workplace, in fact, you should. But should you be inviting them to your big bash, or going on vacation together? Probably not. A company-sponsored outing or party is very different, of course, and in that case, everyone will attend.

- **These suggestions should apply to social media, too.** Connecting on LinkedIn is one thing. Friending and following on other, more personal sites can potentially lead to trouble. If you have a bad day and vent on your personal profile (which you probably shouldn't do, but that's another issue) and you coworkers see it, will that cause problems?

- **If you're tempted by an office romance or hookup, please don't do it** (see chapter 4 for all the reasons why this is a terrible idea).

 Keeping a bit of distance at work does not mean been cool or aloof, much less rude. It simply means not getting too wrapped up in other people's personal affairs. You can be perfectly cordial and warm with those who share the office space—but keep in mind that some barriers are good and healthy.

EXTERNAL MEETINGS CAN BE A GOOD ALTERNATIVE

Most of your office meetings will probably take place on-site and require no more than walking across to the meeting room, or maybe going up or down a floor or two. Sometimes, however, meetings will be held elsewhere. These gatherings may be to meet with clients or another business, or your boss may think that a change of scene will facilitate a better exchange of ideas. Here are some facts about off-site meetings.

- **There are companies that now offer dedicated off-site meeting spaces that rent by the hour.** Your employer may choose to do rent one of these locations on occasion to give everyone a different perspective, take advantage of different technologies, and shake things up a bit. New surroundings can encourage new thinking and get you out of your routine.

- **A change of scene can be nice,** a chance for everyone to get out of the office, maybe get a bit of fresh air, and clear their heads.

- **Sometimes meetings can be rolled into other activities:** a working lunch, a half-day at the park, etc. Think of them as field trips!

- **The same etiquette applies to off-site meetings as to those in your workplace:** arrive a bit early, come prepared

(read any materials beforehand), ask questions, be courteous to others, and engage. If the meeting includes people form outside your company, that is all the more reason to be respectful and attentive. See chapter 1 for more advice on general meeting etiquette.

- **If you are meeting with a client, you want to show your company in the best possible light.** Always be on time and give the other(s) your full attention and courtesy. This is where deals might be made or commitments pledged and honored.

Off-site meetings offer many advantages over the usual and routine meetings in your workplace. If you go prepared and ready, you may find that you even look forward to them!

[
"There is one crucial rule that must be followed in all creative meetings. Never speak first. At least at the start, your job is to shut up."

—WILLIAM GOLDMAN
]

SO, YOU'RE TRAVELING ON A BUSINESS TRIP

At some point, you may be sent on a business trip, for any number of reasons. These can be fun and exciting, but they can also be a hassle. Here are some travel tips to help you make the most of it, avoid fatigue, and present yourself at your best when you arrive.

- **Whether you are traveling domestically or internationally, it's normally assumed that the company will pay for it—but clarify this ASAP.** If your company pays, expect to travel in coach, not business class. Budgets for travel are getting tighter all the time.

- **Obviously, arrive at the airport or train station with plenty of time to check in and get settled.** Make sure to take into account long lines, TSA check, traffic, and other unpredictable factors. Assume that everything will take longer than you want it to, because it probably will!

- **Make sure that you have all travel documents at hand and in order:** your passport or suitable ID, necessary travel or work visas, tickets or booking numbers, etc. Keep a photocopy or a scan of your passport with the number clearly visible, either on your phone, or printed out and kept elsewhere on your person.

- **Make sure that you have travel insurance,** including any necessary health insurance. Don't skip this step!

- **Pack what you need, but don't overdo it.** If you need more formal business and/or evening clothes, bring them, but try to pack things that aren't likely to wrinkle. If possible, bring a carry-on bag only.

- **If you are meeting clients or business associates at the airport on your arrival, it may be advisable to dress more formally,** according to whatever the expectations are. Keep something extra with you on the plane to put on when you arrive.

- **If you are traveling a long distance, prepare for the inevitable jet lag.** Stay hydrated by drinking lots of water; avoid alcohol. Remove your shoes, and take time periodically during the flight to stand up and move around. Stretch and shake out your legs and feet.

- **Again, we assume that your company is putting you up in a hotel.** Take time to familiarize yourself with it and the surrounding area. Do you need a rental car? Or are taxis or ride-shares sufficient? Who pays for these?

- **Be mindful that you're there for business, and no leisure can interfere with your main work.** Though, if your hosts invite you on a social excursion, then by all means, accept.

- **Occasionally, you may have to travel on short notice,** and some of this advice will go out the proverbial airplane window.

Business trips can be rewarding, even fun. You might meet interesting new people, learn new things, or see fascinating new places. Don't shy away from the opportunity to go on one if it comes up!

MONEY BACK! SUBMITTING FOR INVOICES AND REIMBURSEMENTS

Whether when traveling for business or in your day-to-day experiences, you may find that you incur expenses on behalf of your company that you pay for out of your own pocket. This may include meals, car rental, and other such expenses, or perhaps purchasing supplies for a conference or meeting. The good news is that these can often be reimbursed. Here are some tips.

- **According to IRS guidelines, your company should have what is called an "accountable plan," or an "accountable expense plan,"** because this may exempt any reimbursements you receive from taxation. Check with your workplace to make sure that they have a system in place. Some expenses may not be reimbursable, so you'll need to know what is and is not. In any case, IRS regulations and tax laws take precedence over company policies, so make sure you know what the tax obligations are.

- **In order to receive reimbursement, you will need to show that the expenses were directly related to your company and your work** as an employee, and you will have to substantiate your claim by showing the time, place, and amount of the expense. Keep receipts for everything.

- **If your company advances you money ahead of time and you spend more than what they gave you, you may be able to claim further expenses if you provide the information listed above.** If you spend less than the amount you received, you will usually be expected to return the unused amount.

- **Make sure that you put in your claim for reimbursement within a reasonable time.** Within two weeks is normal.

- **Companies will have their own guidelines for invoicing for expenses.** Make sure you follow them exactly, or it may delay your reimbursement.

- **Some companies have what is called a "nonaccountable" plan,** which is simply a set amount put aside, say, $50 a day for meals when traveling. If you go over this amount, you will have to pay the rest yourself. If you don't use it all, the money is yours to keep, but in either case, it is taxable. Check and see what policy your company has.

Most companies are reasonable when it comes to expenses, but policies will vary from business to business. If you know you will be incurring extra expenses for any reason, check in and find you how you can save yourself some money.

GETTING THE MOST OUT OF CONFERENCES

> Business conferences are a common feature of many industries, and the chances that you'll be sent to one sooner or later are good. Quite often, they'll be in another town or city. We've talked about how to make the most of a business trip, but here is some advice for getting the most out of the conference itself.

- **Consider volunteering to contribute.** This may include offering a presentation or a paper, helping to facilitate another session, helping coordinate, and being on the conference committee. All of these things will help you and you company stand out. Always be willing to offer your own help; talk with your employer about what you can do and contact the appropriate conference organizers if you want to get involved.

- **If you've never been to a conference before, check to see if there is an orientation or meeting** for newcomers on the first day or the evening before the full conference starts. These can be invaluable for getting up to speed and getting the most out of the experience.

- **Dress nicely.** You may not have to be too formal, but a little extra effort reflects well on you.

- **If the conference has presentations and papers, try to choose the ones that are most interesting and relevant to you.** It's very possible that you won't be able to attend every session that you'd like, so you'll have to make some trade-offs. Prioritize the ones that seem most meaningful and helpful. Your employer may also request that you attend certain sessions, and these, of course, will take precedence.

- **Take notes, lots of them.** Ask questions. Think of yourself as being back in college. Keep your cell phone off and give your attention to the presenters.

- **Try to connect with speakers that are interesting or important to you.** They're not rock stars and most of them will be more than happy to engage in some further discussion, or at least trade contact information.

- **Conferences are prime places for networking, so make sure you have an ample supply of business cards or other contact information.** Now is not the

time to be reserved! Make sure you keep track of who you meet, the context, and why they're important. Writing a quick note on the back of someone's business card, for example, is a great way to remind yourself of who the person is and what you talked about.

- **Most conferences have evening social events, and it is a good idea to attend one or more.** It's a chance to socialize a bit outside of the work environment, and maybe get to know people in your industry a bit better. The advice about alcohol consumption still applies, however. Drink responsibly and remember that you are representing your company. You may well be there on their dime, so don't do anything that would embarrass them or yourself.

- **Disconnect from your phone and email during the day,** as much as possible, unless there are specific conference happenings listed online that are helpful. It may be that a short text or email is a great way to plan a meetup with someone.

- **After the conference, make the effort to reach out to those you connected with,** such as presenters that resonated with you, and especially potential new clients or customers. The contacts you make at a conference can be long-lasting and lead to greater things. Conferences can be great for learning new things, networking, getting a broader view of your industry, and even having a bit of fun. Go in prepared and with the right attitude, and you'll get the most out of them.

> **"I try to have little or no alcohol when I go to a big conference. Sorry to be a party pooper, but that stuff can regress you really fast, and this is not a good place to regress."**
>
> **—TIMOTHY MORTON**

GOING OUT FOR DRINKS AND SOCIALIZING

Having noted that it's a good idea to differentiate between coworkers and close personal friends, it's still a perfectly good idea to bond with your colleagues in the work environment. Being on good and friendly terms with everyone is essential to making your workplace an enjoyable one, and for group morale and productivity. Socializing with your group on occasion is an excellent way to keep that goodwill. Here are some ways to make the most of it.

- **Your workplace may have a regular, designated day of the week set aside for a bit of team socializing,** or it may be a more occasional outing, out together without any "official" input. It's good to go to these at least some of the time. If you're just too tired, overwhelmed, or not in the mood on one occasion, you can simply decline politely and offer to make it up to them another time.

- **"Going for drinks" can mean just that, going to a bar or restaurant, or it might be a more general term for getting together.** If you don't drink for personal or religious reasons, you can still make the most of these outings. Simply tell your colleagues that you don't drink alcohol, and order juice, soda, water, whatever you prefer. It's your presence, not the alcohol, that is most important.

- **If you do drink, always do so in moderation.** These gatherings are never a time to get drunk and start unloading your grievances about the boss to your colleagues (especially if your boss is there!). Go in with the assumption that your coworkers, and even your boss, are watching, or that news of what you say or do will get back to them.

- **It's a good idea to order food along with your drinks,** to slow down the effects of alcohol.

- **Know your limits and don't exceed them.** Don't do shots! Stick with a drink you can sip over time.

- **Discussions about work will inevitably come up but try not to be negative.** Also, try to steer the conversation away from work at times, and toward something different that isn't controversial (politics is usually a bad idea).

- **If the setup is to buy in rounds, don't neglect to buy when it's your turn.**

- **If your boss is there and offers to buy you a drink, accept,** but again, know your limits, and don't choose the most expensive thing on the menu.

Social and drinking occasions can be fun, a way to get to know your colleagues a bit better, and a good way to wind down after a long week. If you drink, do so in moderation and remember that what you say and do is a reflection on you and on your workplace.

HOW TO SURVIVE THE HOLIDAY PARTY

Ah, the holidays! Deck the halls and make mirth! Except, office parties may be a nightmare of epic proportions, more likely to turn you into a Scrooge than a happy reveller. If you work at a company that throws such an annual bash, here are some ideas for what you can do to make the most of it and maybe even enjoy yourself.

- **The party might be a very casual one, held at a bar, a restaurant, or even in the office. Or it might be a splendid shindig at a fancy hotel, or something similar.** Do your research about the dress code and dress accordingly. Don't show up to a four-star hotel in jeans with holes in them. If you have to go from work straight to the party, bring a change of clothes with you that day. And forget the awful holiday sweater, unless costumes and humor are a part of the festivities.

- **Bring something to share.** This is often expected, but even if not explicitly stated, it's nice to have extra food and drink. Your coworkers will thank you.

- **If you are worried about the alcohol-to-food ratio, make sure to eat a good meal beforehand.** This way, if there are only snacks, you'll be more comfortable, and you won't rely on alcohol to fill an empty stomach. Or, at least, you'll be full and the alcohol won't have the same effect on you. Drink plain old water and stay hydrated.

- **Be careful about overindulging on rich, sweet, and unusual foods,** because the mixture of them may make your stomach regret it later on. Eat strategically and don't binge.

- **Watch how much alcohol you drink, seriously.** Beer, wine, spirits . . . consume them all in moderation. And be aware that the "Christmas punch" is often notoriously alcoholic, even if it's crammed with sugar and fruit juice. A few glasses too many and you may be embarrassing yourself. The same goes for the rum balls and the alcohol-soaked cake. Just keep an eye on it.

- **Keep your conversations with others light and fun.** Even though this is a party, it's not a time to indulge in gossip or negativity. On the other hand, don't just talk about work; people might start to avoid you!

- **Don't take any recreational drugs before or during the party.** Just don't. Whatever you may choose to do in your personal life should not spill over into this kind of gathering. Even though it's a party and a chance to relax, you are still on company time and your behavior is a reflection of you.

- **Nearly 40 percent of people have admitted to hooking up at an office holiday party; don't be one of them.** Your workplace may have specific guidelines about romances and affairs already in place, but even if it doesn't, a drunken hookup could lead to some extremely awkward situations in the days and weeks to follow. There will be gossip, oh yes, there will. And this goes for both women and men: if you engage in sexual behavior while intoxicated, or high, or just feeling horny, even if it seems consensual at the time, you have no idea how the other person will react the next day. Harassment and even assault charges have been filed over misunderstandings. Keep cool and just enjoy the party.

Holiday parties should be fun, and if you follow this advice, yours will be!

CHAPTER 4

WORKPLACE DIFFICULTIES

You'll no doubt hope that your job and workplace environment will be welcoming, cordial, even an enjoyable place to be. You also have every right to feel safe and respected, and to be able to attend to personal needs when the time calls for it. But what happens if something goes wrong, or you encounter a difficult situation? This chapter looks at some of the most common difficult issues that you might face in your workplace and offers advice and solutions to make these problematic times a bit easier.

OFFICE ROMANCES: JUST SAY NO

That cute new receptionist? That awesome new IT person? When you spend a good portion of your week at one place and working with a variety of people, it's not out of the question that someone will catch your eye, if you're single and looking. But is it a good idea to mix personal and professional? We've already advised that keeping some distance between work and your outside life is a good idea, so you might be sad to learn that this goes for office romances as well. Here are some reasons why.

- **Your company might well have a policy against office romances.** This may seem unfair, but they are within their rights to expect certain conduct from their employees. Carrying on a secret romance with a coworker might seem exciting, but if you get caught (and you will), you could both face disciplinary action. At the very least, you may need to disclose that you are dating your coworker.

- **If you decide to ask someone out or date them, the office will talk.** There will be gossip. Spare yourself from being on the receiving end before it even begins.

- **Being infatuated with your coworker in the next cubicle or even in another department might seem exciting and romantic—**but ask yourself if it will distract you from your job. What happens if a work conflict arises and you find yourselves on opposite sides, through no fault of your own? Can you set work boundaries with your partner that are healthy, and treat that person as you would any other colleague?

- **Conversely, what if the two of you have difficulties in your personal relationship, and then have to work together on a project?** That conflict will inevitably spill over into the workplace.

- **Following on from that, what if you break up?** What if it's not amicable? This could cause a big mess at work that will affect your ability to do your job, and it might even make you not want to be there at all. Would you be willing to quit so you didn't have to see that person again? Is your job worth it?

- **If your crush is your boss or supervisor, or conversely someone who works under you, just don't do it, ever.** It's a recipe for disaster.

- **A bit of flirting with a coworker can seem like harmless fun, but be sure of your intentions.** You don't want to give the wrong message if you have no interest in that person beyond flirting; too much of it can cause uncomfortable feelings. If you are overly flirty with someone, even if you think it's harmless, they might not see it the same way. Harassment complaints and worse can result.

It might be tempting to indulge in a romance with an appealing coworker, but most often, the negatives outweigh the benefits, and can lead to a world of trouble. It's far better to keep your romantic life separate, so that you have someone you can go to and be with in your private life, without worrying about work complications.

DEALING WITH A DIFFICULT COWORKER

Unfortunately, there's a decent chance that there's at least one person at your workplace whom you won't get along with. That may not be your fault, or theirs; it's just that sometimes people don't gel. The problem is that you still have to work with them. So, what can you do to make things bearable and prevent conflicts from escalating?

- **Stay calm and don't lose your temper.** Even if you are completely justified in doing so, it will almost always make you look bad.

- **If you comfortable doing so, try to engage the person directly about the issue.** We never know what's going on in someone else's personal life, so there may be any number of circumstances causing this person to be difficult. They may not even be aware that they're causing problems for you. Be respectful and try to see things from their perspective.

- **At the same time, if you do speak, communicate your concerns and what you need.** The person may be more receptive than you think once they understand you.

- **Try to take the high road and be the bigger person.** Yes, that's not easy, but if this person is being difficult to others, it will reflect well on you to rise above it.

- **If the person just seems difficult for the sake of being difficult, try to find out a bit about how they treat others in the office.** It could well be that it's not just you.

- **However, be careful about complaining to coworkers.** News travels fast around the office, and if you tell someone, even someone you trust, there's a chance that it will spread. And then everyone gets dragged in, or even worse, starts taking sides. Leave your complaining for your outside friends and family.

- **If all else fails, speak to your boss.** This should be a last resort, however, when all other attempts to resolve the issue have failed. If you complain too often about other people on the job, you will be seen as the troublemaker. Bring evidence of the problem and how this person's behavior is having a negative impact on your work. Don't just assume that the boss will take your side, however. They may try to work out some compromise.

It's almost inevitable that someone will rub you the wrong way at some point. Following these guidelines will help you navigate the difficulties a little more easily and prevent them from becoming a major source of stress.

DEALING WITH A DIFFICULT BOSS OR SUPERVISOR

Dealing with a difficult coworker is one thing, but what do you do if your supervisor or boss is the one causing you stress and grief? This is a potential nightmare scenario and one that you must approach carefully. Here are some tips.

- **Determine the source of the problem.** Is your boss a micromanager? Always up in your space? Not very good at their job? Narcissistic? Just blatantly mean or condescending? The nature of the problem will affect how you handle it.

- **Try to find out if the problem is with you personally or everyone in the office.** If it's everyone, then you're not alone and it means this person has problems with dealing with people in general. Watch your boss for a few days. If it's just you, however, then the problem is personal. Again, knowing this will determine how you deal with it.

- **What might be motivating your boss to act a certain way?** Are they under pressure from their own supervisors? Is the company having problems? Maybe they are dealing with personal issues of their own. Finding out about these things might not be possible, but it is something to consider.

- **Whatever is happening, try not to let it overly affect your own work; yes, that can be difficult.** But you don't want to give your boss any excuses for begin even more difficult with you. Try not to be defensive. Keep your distance without obviously avoiding them. Be efficient and on time with your work, so that you don't give them anything extra to complain about.

- **Remember that your boss is human, too,** and doesn't know everything. They may not even be very good at their job but got promoted into it.

- **Keep a record of what is happening,** including the incident, the date, and the time. It may be that at some point, your boss will be in trouble for their behavior, and your record will be helpful in higher-ups assessing the problem.

- **If your boss seems approachable, try speaking directly about the problem.** As with coworkers, they may not be aware of their behavior, or they may be dealing with other stresses. It might be possible to clear the air to your mutual satisfaction.

- **If all else fails, and you work in a large enough company, consider requesting a transfer to another department or section.** Just be sure not to name your boss as the only reason you wish to move, and state why you would do well in another department.

The bad boss is a bad dream for a lot of people, but it doesn't have to be the end of the world. Start with these ideas and see if they help resolve your problems.

SIMPLE TRICKS FOR CONFLICT RESOLUTION

In the previous two sections, we looked at how to handle difficult people at work. If you do have the chance to speak with your boss, here are some helpful ideas for how to make that uncomfortable conversation go more smoothly.

- **Don't avoid it.** It may be uncomfortable, but the longer you let it go, the worse things will get. If you need a few days or weeks to assess the situation and gather facts, do so, but then, be ready to work to resolve it.

- **This isn't about winning.** Look for a solution that you can both accept.

- **Agree to meet face-to-face.** This can be uncomfortable, but it's the best way to move things forward. Email and other nonverbal communication can leave someone feeling confused about intentions or tone. Find a time that is acceptable to you both and stick to it.

- **Give each other time to explain differing points of view and where you're coming from.** You might both be surprised that you have more in common that you think. Take time to listen to the other party and be sure that they give you equal time. Communication in a safe and comfortable environment is key here.

- **If necessary, and if your company provides for it, a mediator might be a good idea,** if you both agree to it. This is someone who can help you stay on topic and offer suggestions.

- **Identify the points that you disagree on, as well as the points you do agree on.** Finding points of agreement can help to resolve the conflict.

- **Discuss which area(s) of conflict are most important for you to resolve, and let the other person do the same.** If you have done something wrong, especially if you were not aware of it, own up to it, apologize, and try to do better. However, you have every right to expect this same courtesy from the other person.

- **Try to develop a plan for working through your differences.** This may involve changing behavior, setting up additional meetings to monitor progress, or other ideas that you both agree on.

- **Be sure to stick to any plans or resolutions that you make.** Nothing will change unless you both make a commitment to doing it. Make a commitment to working things out.

- **Further mediation may be called for,** if after all of this, friction remains, or you still can't resolve the issue. Talk with your employer about other solutions.

Workplace conflicts are almost inevitable, but they don't have to be the end of the world. Approach the other party with an open mind, while also standing up for yourself, and always make working things out the main goal.

HOW TO HANDLE INAPPROPRIATE BEHAVIOR

Any number of behaviors at work can be deemed "inappropriate." We'll look specifically at sexual harassment and racism in the next two sections. Here are some thoughts on more general behaviors, and what not to do.

- **It should go without saying to always be on your best behavior at work.** Treat people as you would like to be treated and don't be rude, condescending, or otherwise disrespectful. If you have a disagreement with someone, look for healthy ways to resolve it (see Simple Tricks for Conflict Resolution, pages 111–112).

- **Bullying and intimidation by a boss or a senior employee is never acceptable.** If the techniques for conflict resolution listed above don't work or are not an option, you will have to consider taking it to a higher source in your company.

- **Gossiping is inevitable when groups of people are put together for a periods of time, but try not to engage in it,** and if you see too much of it going on, you might consider taking the person or persons aside and letting them know that their actions might be hurtful. It is not your job to police others' office behavior, of course, so only do this if you feel comfortable and confident doing so. If the gossip is about you, then you have every right to put a stop to it.

- **Making derogatory comments is always unacceptable:** about anyone's appearance, regardless of their gender, race, religion, or position in the company.

- **The same goes for one's personal life, sexual orientation, dating life, or any other information that is no one's business.** If this happens to you, it is worth your time to report it to your supervisor. No company wants to risk legal action due to the misconduct of an employee.

- **If you are called names (i.e., "babe," "sweetie," "honey," etc.), know that this is unprofessional and unacceptable.** If this happens to you, you may have recourse through taking the issue to higher-ups, your boss, or their supervisors. Keep calm and try to explain the situation as clearly as possible, and why it feels offensive or uncalled-for.

- **Office emails should be kept for work-related subjects only.** Do not send anything that seems inappropriate, even if you are only sharing something you received. If you receive an email or communication that feels inappropriate, offensive, or "off," follow the guidelines for conflict resolution and make the time to speak in person to the sender of the email. Express your concerns in a nonconfrontational way and give the person time to respond. Explain why you felt it was inappropriate.

- **Unwanted physical contact of any kind can be grounds for harassment complaints, even if there was no sexual intent.** This includes any kind of unwanted touching, being cornered, someone telling sexual jokes, and making innuendos. See the section on sexual harassment (pages 115–117) for how to handle this.

If you are harassed, you may have recourse through the U.S. Equal Employment Opportunity Commission. See Your Legal Rights and Recourses, pages 126–27.

DEALING WITH SEXUAL HARASSMENT

In this day and age sexual harassment is being taken more seriously, as reports flood the daily news about inappropriate conduct at all levels of society. This is a serious issue, and it deserves to be taken seriously. Sexual harassment violates Title VII of the Civil Rights Act of 1964, and you have legal recourse against it. How should you respond, if such an incident happens to you?

- **First, know that it is your employer's responsibility to ensure that harassment doesn't happen, and to stop it if it does.** You are not responsible if someone harasses you. Employers have a legal obligation to ensure a safe work environment for everyone, and this is not optional.

- **Everyone has different ideas of what they consider acceptable and not acceptable.** This doesn't excuse others' behavior, but we each bring our own level of tolerance to the table. You will know what yours is and what you won't tolerate. Stand firm with that and refuse to be told that you're being "too sensitive" or any other attempts to excuse harassing and abusive behavior.

- **Understand that you have every right to your feelings and if you are harassed, it is not your fault.** It is *not* your fault. It's nothing that you said or did to "lead someone on," it's not what you're wearing, or what you say. You have every right to feel safe and respected, to have your own bodily autonomy, and to feel comfortable in your workplace at all times.

- **Federal law recognizes two types of harassment:** quid pro quo and hostile work environment.

- *Quid pro quo* **is the offer to trade sexual favors for advancement.** This can include hiring, promotions, raises, threats of firing or demotion, and so on.

- *Hostile work environment* **covers anything of a sexual nature that makes you uncomfortable.** This includes actual advances, unwanted touching, unwanted invasion of personal space, sexual jokes (in person or via email), images sent by email (jokes, pornography, etc.), comments about the attractiveness of you or other employees, and so on.

- **Both men and women are harassed, by both men and women.** There is often, though not always, a power dynamic involved. The harasser can be anyone, from a boss to a client or customer. It is never acceptable, regardless of the source.

- **These incidents may leave you angry, confused, embarrassed, or feeling any number of other ways.** This is a normal reaction, and you are fully entitled to your feelings. Again, this is *not* your fault.

- **How you decide to respond is also entirely up to you.** You do have legal recourse in many cases, but there is a lot of fear built into these encounters. You may feel threatened, humiliated, worried that you'll lose your job. Many choose never to come forward, and you have that right. But remember that there are resources available, more so than ever these days. (See the Resources section, page 164.)

- **Please do not hesitate to reach out to friends, family, a therapist, even legal counsel, if you are suffering.** You are not alone.

For more information on what you can do, see Your Legal Rights and Recourses, pages 126–27.

[
"Simple peck-order bullying
is only the beginning of the
kind of hierarchical behavior
that can lead to racism,
sexism, ethnocentrism,
classism, and all the other
-isms that cause so much
suffering in the world."
]

—*OCTAVIA BUTLER*

DEALING WITH RACISM OR OTHER BIASES

Unfortunately, racism and other bigotries are nowhere near being eliminated, much as society might like to tell itself that they are. If you are a member of a minority group (racial, religious, LGBT, etc.), know that discrimination can come in many forms. This is a vast topic that requires far more detail than can be given below, but here is a short guide for what to look out for and how to take action to stand up for your rights.

- **Discrimination of any kind is illegal,** though of course that doesn't stop it from happening. It can be obvious, or more hidden, even institutional. It can come in the form of off-the-cuff remarks or jokes from coworkers or supervisors, being passed over for promotions and recognition, or being unjustly fired. It can be something as simple as being complimented on how well you speak English, or how you are different from other people "like you." While these latter examples may not be intended in a hurtful way, they do represent examples of institutionalized bias.

- **If an incident happens to you or a work colleague, document it.** Take note of the date, time, place, and the individuals involved. Write everything down and keep it in a safe place, away from work. You may be called on at some point to produce evidence and the more detail you have, the better.

- **If you feel comfortable doing so, report any incidents to your boss or supervisor in writing, and keep copies.** Companies should have a zero-tolerance policy regarding racism, and most will want to investigate and eliminate the problem as soon as possible. If nothing is done about it, you may want to consider going over the heads of your immediate superiors, especially if they are a part of it or seem unconcerned.

- **Title VII of the Civil Rights Act of 1964 prohibits racial discrimination in the workplace.** If your company has an HR department, they are required to investigate all complaints in a timely and fair manner. If there is no HR, then it is up to your boss or manager to conduct the investigation. If they don't do so, they are in violation of the law.

- **Reporting incidents can be difficult.** You may be worried about backlash or repercussions, being fired, etc. This is illegal, but that doesn't prevent it from happening. These fears are valid, and only you can determine if reporting is the course of action you should take. Talk with friends, family, and, if it seems appropriate, any coworkers who may have been victims.

- **You can file a complaint with the Equal Employment Opportunity Commission (EEOC),** if you are not sure what you should do, or if you have complained to management and not been satisfied with the result . . . their website has details on what to do (see Resources, page 164).

Racism and other forms of discrimination are vast and complex topics, and no simple guide is going to be able to properly assist you in dealing with the minefield of legal, ethical, and emotional problems that come up around it. Make use of the section on legal rights and recourses (pages 126–27) and the resources section at the back of the book and reach out to anyone that you think can help.

TAKING UNEXPECTED TIME OFF

We go through life hoping and expecting that we'll remain healthy and that our friends and family will also. Unfortunately, things don't always work out that way. You or a loved one may face a medical or other emergency that pulls you away from work for days, weeks, even months. What can you do in this situation?

- **If something happens to a family member and you get notification at work, tell your boss or supervisor right away.** If you need to leave, explain what has happened. It's highly likely that your boss will understand. If not, leave anyway and work the details out later. Your family is your highest priority, not the whims of someone who thinks you should stay and keep working.

- **If you are the victim of an accident or other health problem, it's important that your employer be notified as soon as possible.** Arrange for a friend or loved one to be an emergency contact and to give news, if necessary.

- **You will need to apply for leave under the Family and Medical Leave Act (FMLA).** if you or a family member are facing a crisis that requires you to be away from work for more than a few days.

- **In the United States, the Family and Medical Leave Act covers both medical reasons and pregnancy as reasons for being off work** (see the next section for pregnancy). If you are covered, you may take up to twelve weeks off without fear of losing your job, however, various restrictions apply: you must have worked for your employer for at least one year and for at least 1,250 hours. Also, your company must employ at least fifty people. Twenty-five states have additional coverage or waive some of these requirements. See the Department of Labor website, FMLA page, for more details (see Resources, page 164).

- **Having this time off is not a guarantee that you will be paid for all of it, or even a portion of it.** Policies vary from company to company and you will need to see how much pay, if any, you can receive.

- **Coverage is for serious illnesses or medical conditions that prevent you from working, or for a family member who is ill and needs your care.** This can include being hospitalized for any reason, suffering from a chronic illness, getting treatment for addiction, mental health issues, and so on. If you are in the military reserves and are deployed, you may also qualify for this protection.

- **It is normally required to give thirty days' notice of your expected absence,** but obviously, in the case of emergencies (accidents, sudden problems, or relapses), this is not possible. Notify as soon as you can and provide letters from your doctor or caregivers if your employer requests them.

- **If you qualify, your employer is not permitted to deny you leave, retaliate, fire, or demote you, or do anything else that would prevent your return.** As noted, you may not qualify for compensation during your absence, and you are not immune from being laid off as part of a company restructuring (or whatever reason they give), especially if you were due to be laid off, anyway.

Medical emergencies and crises can be among the most stressful things that we will ever endure. No matter how hard we try to stay healthy, bad things can happen. Expect the best, but always be prepared in case something does happen.

GETTING THE MOST OUT OF PARENTAL LEAVE

You're expecting a child? Congratulations! But you also work full time. What happens now?

- **Unlike a majority of countries, the United States does not have a federal law governing standard maternity leave lengths or pay.** About 60 percent of companies offer twelve weeks (the minimum by law, see below), and more than 30 percent offer more time than that, but not all of this might be paid. In fact, less than 60 percent of businesses pay for at least a portion of that time; many don't pay at all. You will need to check with your own company early on to find out what their policies are.

- **In the U.S., most women receive no government payments, and instead rely on the Family and Medical Leave Act (FMLA),** which protects their jobs for twelve weeks. This act guarantees that you will be able to return to your job without being fired or being forced to take a pay cut. However, the act only applies to companies with fifty employees or more, and only if you have worked there for a minimum of 1,250 hours during the last year. It's frustrating and complicated, and you will have to refer to the Department of Labor website (FMLA page) for more details (see Resources, page 164).

- **Twenty-five states have supplemental additions to FMLA that extend the period beyond twelve weeks or lower the minimum number of employees required.** Again, check the Department of Labor website for details and see if your state participates.

- **FMLA laws apply both to natural birth and to adoption and fostering.**

- **While you cannot be fired and are protected from retaliation for leaving, company layoffs due to downsizing and such are not subject to this law,** so in theory, you could still lose your job while on leave.

- **Under FMLA, you are required to give at least thirty days' notice of your intent to take leave**, though most will choose to do so long before that.

- **When to take your leave will be up to you in consultation with your doctor.** You may want to take a bit of time before the birth to be prepared. If you have no complications and have a fairly reliable due date, you should give your employer at least thirty days' notice for when you intend to take the actual time off as a courtesy, even if you have previously given notice in compliance with the law.

- **You are not obligated to take time off right after giving birth, if you don't wish to,** and can use those twelve weeks at any time up to a year after doing so.

- **You may be able to extend your time away,** depending on the state you live in and your employer's willingness to allow it. Check with FMLA and your employer's guidelines well in advance.

These few bits of advice only scratch the surface. You will need to discuss things in detail with your employer and study up on how federal and state laws apply to you. Good luck and congratulations!

WHEN YOU'VE BEEN LAID OFF OR FIRED

> We hope that our work experiences will not only be satisfying, but long-lasting. When we go into a new company, we may expect to be there for years, perhaps even to make a career out of it. The reality is that changing careers is becoming ever more common (with many people doing it several times over the course of their working lives), and businesses sometimes simply cease to be, downsize, or get swallowed up by competitors. The result is that you may find yourself out of a job, through no fault of your own. But what if it is your fault and you get fired?

- **Understand the distinction between getting laid off and getting fired.** Getting fired has to do with poor work performance, misconduct at work, always being late, taking too much time off, violating nondisclosure agreements (NDAs), etc. All of these are a result of your personal actions. Getting laid off is usually due to the company downsizing or cutting costs, going out of business, or some similar reason that you are not responsible for.

- **In the United States, people generally work under the concept of being "at-will" employees,** meaning that the employer can let you go at any time and is under no obligation to provide a reason for your termination. In practice, it's likely you will be told, especially if it's not your fault.

- **If you are laid off, check to see if you are owed severance pay.** Also, be sure to find out where to collect your final paycheck and see if you have any additional money coming to you in the form of overtime, sick leave, or vacation pay. Be sure that you receive everything that is coming to you!

- **Being fired or being laid off will make a difference if you file for unemployment insurance.** Generally, to qualify for insurance, you have to show that you were let go through no fault of your own. Your former boss might even be willing to write a letter in support of your claim. If you've been fired, you probably will not qualify for insurance, unless you can show that you were unjustly terminated, such as because of discrimination, being a whistleblower for illegal activity, etc.

- **Check on the status of your benefits, such as health coverage and other perks.** Some of them might continue for a while, some might not. This also goes for your 401(k) or any other retirement plan.

- **See to it that you gather a few letters of recommendation from colleagues or your supervisors,** if your termination was not due to anything acrimonious. Most will probably be more than happy to help you out.

- **If you have been fired, try to understand why.** Was it for a legitimate reason? Did you violate a company policy or act inappropriately? Did you make an honest mistake? You will need to use this painful time as a learning experience. However, if you suspect that you have been wrongfully fired (there are number of reasons this may have happened), you may be able to file a wrongful termination claim.

Losing your job for any reason is stressful and upsetting, so use this advice to help navigate what to do next.

YOUR LEGAL RIGHTS AND RECOURSES

> If you find yourself in a situation where you are facing harassment of any kind, abuse, threats, you witness illegal activities, or must deal with any other problems that might be beyond your company's ability (or willingness) to solve, what can you do? Here is a list of resources and helpful suggestions. Websites are listed in the Resources section, page 164.

- **The Equal Employment Opportunity Commission (EEOC) exists to allow people to file complaints about sexual harassment, racist activity, and several other forms of discrimination,** including based on age, disability, religious beliefs, national origin, and other categories. Their website gives details on the proper procedures to follow if your company engages in these practices, ignores your complaints or concerns, or you experience retaliation or wrongful termination.

- **The U.S. Department of Labor (DOL) maintains standards for employee safety, wages, hours, and other such concerns.**

- **Different states can have their own employment laws, which do not overrule federal law,** unless they are stricter and protect workers' rights better (they can't be less protective), such as a higher minimum wage, granting longer leave times, and so on. Check with your individual state's laws and see what applies. Cornell University Law School maintains a listing of each state's labor department website.

- **The National Labor Relations Board (NLRB) monitors and assists in employees' right to form labor unions.** Several states have enacted "right to work" laws which favor companies who want to fire employees as at-will workers and for trying to unionize, among other things. However, the right to form unions is protected under the National Labor Relations Act. It is illegal for your boss to fire you (or threaten to fire you) for forming or joining a union, nor can they favor employees who don't support unionizing, close your place of employment, or try to bribe you with a higher wage if you agree not to join. If you experience any of these violations, gather your evidence, and contact the NLRB.

- **Legal Aid at Work offers free online resources** for fact sheets, legal advice, litigation, and policy advocacy, as well as news stories about employment law. This is an excellent resource if you are in need of legal advice and representation.

HOW TO RECOGNIZE BURNOUT AND WHAT TO DO ABOUT IT

> You may have loved your work when you started. A year ago, five years ago, even more, it was exciting, thrilling, and you felt valuable and valued. But now, things seem to be changing. It's not the way it used to be. Maybe you're bored, maybe you're starting to resent having to go in, maybe everything just seems unimportant or overwhelming. You may be facing burnout. Here are some of the signs and what to do about them.

- **First of all, understand that it's not just you.** The World Health Organization classifies burnout as a genuine health issue. In 2019, WHO noted that burnout is a "syndrome conceptualized as resulting from chronic workplace stress that has not been successfully managed." You may feel exhausted, have no interest in what you're doing, and no longer do your job well.

- **There are many key emotional symptoms of job burnout,** including lack of interest in work or going to work, not caring about what happens on the job anymore, not putting in the effort that you once did, feeling angry or resentful about being there, and being irritated with your boss simply because they exist.

- **There are also physical symptoms** you may notice that you're increasingly tired, and may be dealing with other symptoms, including insomnia, gastrointestinal issues, headaches or body aches, chest pain, dizziness, and more head colds or other periodic sicknesses. It is important to see a doctor to rule out any other causes of your symptoms. But if everything else seems normal enough, you may indeed be suffering from job burnout.

- **In order to successfully treat the problem, you will have to examine what might be the underlying conditions and causes.** These could be just about anything, and only you can determine what really is getting to you. Does the problem originate with you? Are you a perfectionist? Do you want to please everyone? Both of these takes can quickly leave you feeling burned out, because you'll never meet your own standards. It's OK to ease up a bit and realize that everyone has limits and makes mistakes.

- **On the other hand, are you dealing with external stresses?** Do you have a boss or coworker who is a bully? Are you facing discrimination or harassment? These are genuine concerns that are addressed in some of the other sections in this chapter.

- **Perhaps your workload is simply too great.** If you volunteered to take on more work than you can handle (a common cause of burnout), perhaps it's time to ease off a bit. If you were assigned more work than you can handle, there is no shame in talking with your boss about how to better manage it.

- **Taking a little time off (a few days or a week) might help in the short term.** Have you not had a vacation in two years? Now is the time. But often the underlying causes of burnout are still there, and you may return to your job feeling a bit better, only to fall back into the same situation a few weeks later.

- **You'll have to ask yourself other questions, such as what your life and career goals are.** Is your workplace no longer satisfying as it relates to these? Are you yearning for a change of career? These are the big questions that only you can answer. But know that career changes are increasingly common, and more and more people are trying to discover what the best fit is for them. Your burnout may be a way of nudging you to change directions and take some new steps.

Job burnout is a serious problem and a recognized health issue. Don't treat it lightly or assume it's just a simple problem that will go away. Ignoring it will likely make it worse in the long run.

GETTING READY TO MOVE ON

Sometimes, the writing is just on the wall. You come to the realization that your job is just not a good fit, it's holding you back, or any number of other problems. How will you know when it's time to make that break? Here are some of the key signs.

- **You're generally unhappy with what you are doing, beyond everyday stresses and problems.** You don't enjoy being into the workplace anymore, and perhaps it's a slog to even make yourself go. Once there, maybe you find yourself procrastinating and avoiding work or your coworkers. Maybe you find yourself complaining about your job to your friends all the time.

- **Your health is suffering.** Whether physical or mental, if you're noticing a decline in your health, the number of hours you sleep, or a need to take more sick days off, it might be a sign that your job is taking a toll on you. If you're resorting to more alcohol or other substances to cope, you definitely need to reassess your situation. No job is worth losing your health over.

- **You might feel that you are overqualified** for what you're doing, or that you have no room to advance any further than you already have with this particular company. Perhaps your skills and knowledge aren't a good fit, and maybe the work is too easy and you're just bored.

- **You are unhappy with your current salary and other compensation or work arrangements,** and there doesn't seem to be a way to resolve it to the mutual satisfaction of both you and your company. Sometimes companies have tight budgets, but other times, they're just being tightwads. Is there a genuine reason you can't work from home once every two weeks if you need to, or are they just being stubborn? If they don't really value you, what should you stay?

- **The workplace environment is stressful, toxic, or harassing.** If you have experienced negativity, hostility, harassment, or retaliation from your boss or coworkers, and there doesn't seem to be a way to fix the problem, it might be time to consider leaving.

- **There is a high turnover in your workplace.** This may indicate that others feel the same way, and the overall structure of the workplace just isn't right for a lot of people.

- **The company itself is going through turmoil and restructuring.** This may be a normal part of its growth, or it may indicate that there are deeper problems. If you are hearing rumors that it may be going out of business or being absorbed by another company, it would be a good idea to keep your eyes open for other opportunities.

- **Headhunters and recruiters are approaching you.** This may mean nothing, but it may mean that your industry is especially "hot" right now, and you might be welcome elsewhere for more money and a better overall experience. Keep your ear to the ground and research what then hiring trends are.

Obviously, just giving notice and leaving may not be an option. Bills, rent, and other expenses don't go away, and you may be stuck in your place of employment for a while before you can make an exit and a quick transition to another company or workplace. But if you are experiencing several of these points on a regular business, it's probably a good idea to think about your long-term plans and start investigating whether another situation would be better for you.

[**"Remembering that I'll be dead soon is the most important tool I've ever encountered to help me make the big choices in life. Because almost everything— all external expectations, all pride, all fear of embarrassment or failure— these things just fall away in the face of death, leaving only what is truly important."**]

—STEVE JOBS

Business is increasingly a global undertaking and foreign markets are as important, if not more so, than domestic ones. If you work for a company that has any international standing (or wishes to have it), it's likely that you will be dealing with representatives from foreign countries at one time or another, whether they are visiting you, or you are sent as part of a team to visit them. Etiquette and conduct vary from nation to nation and culture to culture, but there are some behaviors that are vital to do and not do to present yourself and your company in the best way. This chapter looks at some of the most important rules of conduct for business with some key countries that you might work with in the future. These are general guidelines, and it's always a good idea to take the time to read up in more detail about your chosen country and its culture, but these lists will be enough to get you started.

HOW TO SAY HELLO IN TWO DOZEN LANGUAGES

Learning a few phrases of your host's country or culture can be an invaluable way of making a good first impression and beginning to forge connections and networks that might last a lifetime. Don't automatically assume that your hosts or clients speak English. They may, but your efforts will still be appreciated. The only way to properly learn a language is by hearing and repeating it, but here are simple greetings in multiple languages to get you started. Be aware of the differences between spelling and pronunciation and seek out videos and other tutorials to help you. These are formal versions of greetings, which you should always use instead of informal. Say these along with the person's name and title (if appropriate).

Arabic
As-sal m 'alaykum (ahs-sahlahm 'ah-leh-koom): hello (literally "Peace be upon you")

Bengali
nômoshkar (naw-mo-shkar): hello (for Hindus)

assalamualaikum (ahs-sah-lahmoo-ah-lay-koom), or *salam* (sah-lahm): hello (for Muslims, literally "Peace be upon you")

Chinese (Cantonese)
néih hóu (nay hoe): hello (literally "Are you well?")

Chinese (Mandarin)
nın hað (nĕen how): hello (literally "Are you well?")

Danish
goddag (goo-day): good day

Finnish
hyvää päivää (hoo-vah pai-vah): good day

French
bonjour (bohn-zhoor): good day

German
guten tag (goo-ten tahk): good day

Greek
ya sas (yah-sas): hello (honorific plural)

kaliméra (kah-lee-meh-rah): good morning

kalispéra (kah-lee-spare-a): good afternoon

Hindi
namaste (nah-mah-steh): hello (literally "I bow to you")

Indonesian
selamat siang (suh-lah-maht see-ahng): good day

selamat pagi (suh-lah-mat pah-gee): good morning

selamat sore (suh-lah-mat sor-ee): good afternoon

Italian
buon giorno (bwohn johr-noh): good morning

buon pomeriggio (bwohn poh-mer-ree-jee-oh): good afternoon

Japanese
konnichiwa (kohn-nee-chee-wah): good afternoon/hello

ohay gozaimasu (oh-hi-oh goh-zai-mas): good morning

Korean
annyeoung haseyo (an-nyee-ong hah-seh-yo): hello

Malay
selamat pagi (se-lah-maht pah-gee): good morning

selamat petang (se-lah-maht pe-tahng): good afternoon

Norwegian
god dag (goo dahg): hello good day

Portuguese
olá (oh-lah): hello

Russian
zdravstvuyte (zdrahst-vooy-tyeh): hello

Spanish
hola (oh-lah): hello

buenos días (bwe-nohs dee-ahs): good morning

buenas tardes (bwe-nahs tahr-dehs): good afternoon

Swahili
shikamoo (shee-kah-mu): hello (literally "I respect you"; said to an elder or someone of senior rank)

hujambo (hoo-jahm-boh): how are you? (somewhat less formal)

Swedish
god dag (goo-dah): good day

Turkish
merhaba (mehr-hah-bah): hello

Yoruba
ek'aro (eh-kahr-roh): good morning

e kasan (eh-kahr-sahn): good afternoon

Vietnamese
chào ch (chow chee): hello (addressing an older or ranking woman)

chào anh (chow ahn): hello (addressing an older or ranking man)

HOW TO HAVE IMPECCABLE BUSINESS ETIQUETTE IN TEN COUNTRIES OR REGIONS

In your travels, you will sometimes be going to countries and cultures that have very different customs and traditions. Whether it is a business trip or a transfer to a foreign branch, it is good to understand some of the details of cultural norms that may not be your own. While the basic rules of politeness and good manners are almost universal, there are some specifics in different countries which will present you and your company in a good light. Showing that you have taken the time to learn about and respect local customs will also demonstrate that you take your new colleagues seriously and are ready to do business with them. That respect will be reciprocated and make your working relationships much easier. Remember that people are individuals, and not every one of these rules and customs will apply to everyone you meet.

Here is a list of ten top countries and regions you might be doing business with, and some of the cultural differences you may encounter.

CHINA AND HONG KONG

China is an economic powerhouse that companies all over the world are eager to do business with. If your company does any international business at all, there is a decent chance that some of it will be with a Chinese company. If you are selected to visit or even to work at a branch, there are some very important cultural practices that you should be aware of. Some of these practices will be similar to those for Japan (see below).

- **An important concept in Chinese business culture (and culture in general) is the concept of "saving" or "gaining" face.** This is essentially reputation and avoiding embarrassing others. This is critical to being able to do business with Chinese companies and people. Never criticize others or expose flaws. Be complimentary and respectful, and you will gain or save face.

- **Gifts are generally not exchanged among business colleagues,** and in some instances are even frowned on, since they could imply a bribe.

- **Business attire should always be conservative and traditional.** Men should wear traditional suits and ties, and women should wear pantsuits—not low-cut tops or short skirts. Dark colors are most acceptable, but here are a few extra pieces of color information: white is the color of mourning, so plain white shirts are not the best choice, especially if you are attending a wedding or some other celebratory event. Red is considered lucky, so a red tie or a red blouse would be welcome, but don't overdo it. Blue is a neutral color, but more associated with masculinity. Yellow is best avoided.

- **Greetings traditionally were made with a bow,** but in recent decades, the handshake or a handshake is increasingly more common. If you do receive a bow, however, be sure to return it, and lower your eyes when bowing. Follow the lead of others. Hierarchy and seniority are very important, and you will greet those of the highest rank first. Titles are also important, and you will use these in combination with someone's last name. You may well hear someone greet you by giving their company's name first, followed by their last name, and then their first name.

- **No other body contact beyond the handshake is acceptable,** and the Chinese do not tend to use their hands when talking, so try not to do so yourself.

- **Decide beforehand how your own company's hierarchy is structured,** so that your hosts can greet you appropriately.

- **In Hong Kong especially, many business people have adopted Western names for ease of communication.** This is a normal practice, so don't be surprised by it.

- **For business cards, print your information in English on one side and Chinese on the other.** Clearly state your professional title. Hand your card to the most senior individual first, holding it with your thumbs and forefingers and presenting it Chinese side up. Inspect any cards you receive and place them in a dedicated holding place that is *not* your wallet or purse.

- **Determine beforehand if you need a translator for any business meetings.** This will be essential and not something you can arrange at the last minute. If a member of your team speaks fluent Chinese (Mandarin), you're in good shape. In Hong Kong, English is commonly spoken, though making the effort to speak some Cantonese will always be appreciated.

- **Punctuality for meetings and other gatherings is essential.** Being late is rude and disrespectful, so always make the effort to be on time or preferably early.

- **A bit of small talk before the meeting is normal and accepted.** Topics such as food, the arts, and the weather are all good. Avoid politics (especially Tibet and Taiwan, and more recently Hong Kong) and personal questions.

- **When entering a meeting room, those of the highest rank will enter first, followed in order by the others.** As a guest, you may be allowed or expected to enter with the high-ranking members of the group, but follow their lead and wait for their invitation to do so. Don't sit down until the host does.

- **The meeting will probably be very structured.** Come prepared, and make sure that you have clear, well-written, and well-designed handouts, if you need these. Prepare facts and figures to back up your claims. Do not rely on bluster or salesmanship; these will not impress anyone. Negotiations over sales and business deals can take a long time, so be patient and don't rush things. A "yes" might simply mean that someone agrees with you, while "no" is rarely used. You should avoid it as well.

- **At the end of a meeting, it is customary for the Chinese to leave first, from highest-ranking to lowest,** though in some instances the order is reversed. Observe the protocol and leave when you are expected to.

- **A business meal may not actually involve business while eating.** You will be seated according to rank, with senior people being seated first. There may be a dozen or more courses, so eat sparingly and expect to be served some unusual dishes you are not used to seeing. If you are a vegetarian who does not want to eat frog, tripe, or insects, explain to your host ahead of time to avoid embarrassment. Some suggest mentioning that you follow a Buddhist diet, as this is vegetarian and understood. Don't begin eating before others, and always leave a small portion of food in your plate, otherwise you may give the impression that you are still hungry or that your hosts didn't feed you enough.

- **Invitations to drink are essential, as you will use this time to build business relationships (also known as "guanxi").** You really can't get out of these, and in fact your host may even see how much alcohol you can handle! Be sure to eat before attending. If you don't drink alcohol at all, make up a medical excuse for why you can't drink.

- **Tips at a meal or drinking place are considered insulting.** Don't leave them.

- **Be careful about certain numbers.** Eight is considered very lucky, so packaging your presentations in groups of eight bullet points, eight numbered paragraphs, etc., will look very good. Conversely, the number four is avoided, because the Chinese word for it also sounds like the word for "death." Avoid using it in your presentations and other material.

FRANCE

The French sometimes have an (unfair) reputation for rudeness, but this is less to do with national character and far more to do with misunderstandings about behavior and social norms. In fact, politeness is highly valued in France, and negative reactions to foreigners are more often as a result of perceived rude behavior on the part of outsiders. Remember to be polite and you will do fine.

- **Learning to speak even a little bit of the language will go a long way.** With French, it really is important to listen to the sounds and get them in your head; French is not spoken like it is written! Try to start every conversation with a little French, even if the conversation then drifts into English. Making the effort reflects well on you.

- **Address others as "Monsieur" or "Madame."** This small bit of extra formality is still very valued. Introduce yourself by both your first and last names.

- **Shake hands at introductions** but avoid an overly firm or aggressive handshake. Keep it light!

- **A somewhat more formal style of dress is also appreciated and even expected.** The French are masters of style and haute couture, of course, and this is reflected in the business attire of men and women. Think dark colors and conservative looks and cuts. Your willingness to dress up a bit more will make a good impression.

- **Carry a business card with English on one side and French on the other.** If you are being interviewed for a French job, offer the interviewer your card, French side up.

- **If you are working for a French company (short or long term), greet your colleagues with a friendly "bonjour" each day.** Respect the personal space of others, but understand that French culture can include more physical, cheek-to-cheek air-kisses, or "faire la bise," for example. These are exchanged by all genders, and are considered the epitome of politeness. This greater level of physical expression is in no way meant as or considered harassment.

Bonjour

- **Avoid talking about your personal life or asking colleagues about theirs.** Keep professional and personal separate. However, the arts, food and wine, sports, and even philosophy are all fair game, and the discussions can become quite spirited! Opinions on politics and religion are, as usual, best left unspoken.

- **Make the effort to be on time for interviews, meetings, business lunches, social events,** and so on, but understand that the French don't view lateness with the same horror as some cultures do. Your guest might arrive to a business lunch ten minutes late and offer no apology. This is not meant to be rude; it's just an aspect of the culture. This loose interpretation of scheduling will be more noticeable the farther south you travel in France.

- **Try not to bother people with calls, emails, or texts during the lunch break** (typically 12:00 p.m. to 2:00 p.m.). Also, don't schedule meetings then, unless it is specifically a lunch meeting in a restaurant or cafe.

- **Avoid being overly assertive or aggressive when making pitches or sales,** and don't push for an immediate decision.

- **If engaging in written correspondence, be sure to reread and correct.** Have a native speaker review your work if you are not comfortable with your French.

- **In French,** "vous" is the formal version of "you" when addressing someone. Always use it. Always. "Tu" is the informal version, reserved for loved ones, close friends, and families. French businesses can put a great deal of emphasis on hierarchies, and maintaining the formal address is always a good idea.

- **With business meetings, be on time and confirm** they are happening a day in advance. Learn what is expected language-wise. They may be comfortable meeting in English, but if not, you will be expected to use French. If you are not comfortable enough doing so, be sure that someone fluent is present to represent your company.

- **Be aware that during meetings, you may be asked some very direct questions.** This is not rude; they merely want to get to the heart of the issue.

- **If meeting for a business dinner or lunch, leave your hands on the table,** not in your lap.

- **If you empty your wineglass, it will be refilled.** Leave a bit in it if you've had enough.

- **Business is most often discussed after the meal is finished.** Be patient.

- **Gift-giving between business associates is not a common practice.** If you wish to thank someone, invite them to dinner, coffee, or even a glass of wine.

GERMANY

Germans have a reputation for being efficient, on time, and accurate. While of course these are stereotypes, the German business world does run at a level of efficiency that is impressive and should be respected. Here is a list of dos and don'ts.

- **Offer a short but firm handshake while maintaining eye contact during an introduction.** Use last names and titles when addressing others. Try to maintain eye contact when talking and keep your hands out of your pockets. Shake hands when meeting and again at the end of an event such as a business meeting.

- **Always knock on doors before entering.**

- **You may have heard jokes about German efficiency, but punctuality really does matter.** Always be on time or early for interviews, business meetings, dinners and other social engagements. Even being five to ten minutes late can look rude or unprofessional, so if you are going to be late, call ahead and let someone know. Your time and everyone else's is respected and you are expected to offer the same respect in return.

- **Perhaps the only thing valued more than time is accuracy.** If you are working on a project, it must be done right.

- **Meetings tend to be well-organized and stick to the agenda.** Accept that and don't deviate from the set topics, unless invited by the head of the meeting to do so.

- **Bring your business cards with you and be prepared to hand them out.** It is not necessary to have them translated into German. Most Germans speak very good English.

- **With that being said, do not presume to just go about addressing everyone in English right off the bat.** It is polite and courteous to learn a few German phrases and greetings, even if only to explain that you don't speak German well.

- **German business demeanor tends to be quite direct, so expect a lot of questions,** but don't press for fast decisions if you are making a sale. Back up everything you offer with graphs, charts, and other evidence.

- **Dress tends toward conservative and dark for both women and men.** Men should avoid brightly colored ties and women should not wear too much makeup.

- **As always, avoid personal topics** such as religion, income, and family, but sports, culture, and beer are all quite acceptable.

- **Respect personal space** and don't touch anyone except for the handshake.

- **If you are attending a business dinner, wait for your host to initiate everything and follow their lead.** The host is also expected to pay for the meal, so there is no need to offer, and in fact it can make you look rude if your press the issue.

INDIA

Business culture in India can be thought of as a blend of its own traditions with influences from British practices. Some things will seem familiar, while others may be unknown. Here is a short guide to the basics.

- **The greeting is often a handshake.** This is most true in cities and "Westernized" settings. In rural and/or more traditional places, it may be considered improper for men and women to shake hands, so be mindful of this and follow the lead of your hosts. In these same areas, some may greet you with the word Namaste ("nah-mah-stay"), either during the handshake or when touching their palms together. Either of these actions may be accompanied by a slight bow. It is acceptable and polite to reciprocate this gesture. A slight bow when shaking hands with a senior businessperson is also acceptable everywhere. Greet the oldest and most senior members of any group first.

- **Other than the handshake, avoid touching anyone,** though you will sometimes see Indian men pat each other on the back as a gesture of friendship and support.

- **Address all people by their title and last name.** Don't use first names unless given permission to do so.

- **In India, as in parts of the Middle East, the left hand is seen as "unclean,"** so don't offer your left hand to shake someone's or use it during eating, even if you are left-handed. Don't use it to offer someone a business card, a drink, money, food, etc., or accept them.

- **Be careful about showing the soles of your feet or shoes.** Don't cross your legs so that your soles are visible and try not to point your feet at anyone. It's best to keep both feet flat on the ground. If you happen to accidentally touch someone else with your feet, apologize. Don't point at anything with your index figure; gesture with your whole hand, if you need to.

- **Your business cards can be in English and should be presented with both hands** (held between thumbs and index fingers), with the text facing the recipient for ease of reading. If you receive a card, thank the giver and examine it. Your basic information is fine, but if you have a higher degree, it's worth putting that information on your cards (M.A., Ph.D.), as it will earn you respect.

- **In India, it is not considered rude to be a few minutes late** for a meeting, lunch, or other gathering, though it won't hurt for you to be on time, and many Indian businesses are now being stricter about punctuality.

- **It is acceptable to bring a small gift to your business hosts.** Sweets are always a good option.

- **At a meeting, don't dive right into the business at hand.** A bit of small talk beforehand is fine and may even include a few innocuous questions about family and such.

- **Business attire is conservative**. Men should wear Western business suits, and women should wear trouser suits or long skirts. Do not wear short skirts or have your shoulders displayed.

JAPAN

You may have heard about (or feared) the legendary complexities of Japanese business etiquette, but they're not that scary or difficult. Once you've spent a bit of time in Japan, you'll get the hang of things pretty easily. Take your cues from others and ask if in doubt, and you'll do fine.

- **Learning a few Japanese phrases shows courtesy and respect, but is not essential.** No one will be offended if you stick to English.

- **It's customary to bow when greeting, though your hosts may offer their hands to shake instead.** Shake hands firmly but not vigorously. If someone bows to you, return the bow. Keep your back straight and gaze in front of you. Men keep their hands at their sides, and women often clasp their hands in front of them. The lower that you bow, the more respect you are showing. *Never* put your hands into your pockets during an introduction; it tells your hosts that you are bored!

- **Business cards are an important part of corporate and business identity in Japan.** If representing your company, bring at least one hundred with you. They should be double-sided, one side in English, the other in Japanese, with the same design on both sides. When presenting your card, offer it with both hands, Japanese side up. When receiving a card, take it with both hands and thank the person giving it to you.

- **Don't stuff cards you receive into your wallet or simply discard them,** much less leave them behind; have a separate card case on hand to put them in. Don't bend, fold, or write on them. If you're at a table, leave the card(s) out on the table for a while. Follow others for when to put them away.

- **Give your card to the senior member first,** and work down the line from there.

- **Before a business meeting, call one hour in advance to ensure that the meeting is still happening;** arrive early (at least ten to fifteen minutes) and fully prepared. Wait to be seated at the meeting table until you are offered a chair. As a guest, you may be seated with senior members. If offered tea, wait until your host takes a sip first before drinking your own.

- **Have an interpreter present at business meetings,** and offer a printed Japanese version in a handout. This goes for slides as well. Take a lot of notes, since these will be referred to later on.

- **Men can wear essentially the same business attire as in America or Europe,** but don't wear an all-black suit with a white shirt and black tie, since this combination is reserved for funerals. Darker suit colors are more common in winter, while lighter gray is more common in spring and summer, though if your trip is short, wear what colors you have. In more traditional workplaces, men wear their hair short and are clean-shaven, so if you are going to work for such a company, bear this in mind.

- **Unfortunately, women in Japan have more difficulties, with both dress codes and the business world in general.** If dealing with more traditional companies, you as a woman may feel you are not taken seriously, or at best are misunderstood. This can be frustrating and unfortunately, it's still a part of Japanese business culture. But when presenting yourself as professional in business environments, here are some dress-code guidelines: wear your hair tied back, favor trouser suits or skirts below the knee, dress in colors that are not too bright, and keep perfumes and scents to a minimum.

- **Don't make small talk, especially about personal and private things, such as family life.** This will likely make your Japanese colleagues uncomfortable; such topics are reserved for close friends. Avoid touching and violating personal space. Don't pat someone on the back, touch their arm, or similar actions; it's too forward.

- **However, if you are invited to someone's home, it is a great honor, and you should always accept,** even if you have to rearrange your own plans. Remove your shoes in a home (you'll get house slippers), and there may be a separate set of slippers to wear to the bathroom. If in doubt, ask.

- **Business is sometimes conducted over drinks, and if you are invited to go along, act accordingly.** Never say negative things about any of your colleagues or even your company's competitors.

- **As in China, the concept of "saving face" is very important,** so act accordingly.

- **If you are given a gift, thank the giver and set it to one side.** Gifts are meant to be opened in private, unless your host wants you to open it right then. If you are giving a gift, expect this same response. Also, try to avoid gifts that contain the numbers four or nine (a set of four teacups, for example). In more traditional circles, these numbers are considered unlucky.

- **Don't blow your nose in public** (excuse yourself and go to a restroom), never point at someone, and never mention someone's mistake or that they are wrong. All of these things are rude and disrespectful.

LATIN AMERICA

For purposes of this section, "Latin America" refers to every country from Mexico to Argentina. While these are different nations with different cultures and languages, there are some similarities that you will notice among them. Be sure to take time to read up on the individual country or countries you will be visiting.

- **Do *not* refer to yourself as an "American."** Technically, everyone in both North America and South America is an "American." The co-opting of this word to mean "from the United States" is not looked on with favor. Say that you're from the United States ("Estados Unidos"), or even better, mention which state and city you are from.

- **While discussion of family is off-limits in some cultures, there is a general appreciation for the subject in Latin American countries.** Be prepared to show photos of your loved ones and to talk about them and yourself. This is not seen as intrusive; it is a way of establish rapport and bonding, important to building a business relationship.

- **Time is generally viewed in a more relaxed manner.** While you should still strive to be on time for meetings and appointments, just in case, accept that lateness is the norm, and you might be waiting a while. For more social events, people will usually arrive a half hour (or more) later than the agreed-on time. This holds true even if you are going to someone's house on an invite. You will not be seen as rude for arriving at 7:30 to 7:45 if the agreed-on time was 7:00. At restaurants, dinners often start late (9:00 p.m. or later) and can go past midnight.

- **Greet new people with a firm handshake and a smile.** There might also be an air-kiss or kiss on the cheek. There is a greater sense of comfort in being in each other's space and in physical contact and casual touching. Try not to be offended by this or to pull away from it, as this might be seen as rude. It's a part of their culture and is not meant to be harassing.

- **Take the time to learn a bit of Spanish or Portuguese, and don't assume that everyone speaks English.** The younger generations are more likely to speak English well, but with older and more senior people, this might not be the case.

- **Your business attire should be sharp and formal.** The smarter you are dressed, the more likely you will be taken seriously. Women may feel at a slight disadvantage, since the number of women in high-ranking business positions is fewer, though that is changing.

- **The business meeting is still the place to get things done, but again, the approach to time may be more casual than you are used to.** Things may run over or take as long as necessary to wrap up. It's often a good idea to try to schedule meetings in the morning.

- **Accept invitations to social engagements, even if it's just coffee or drinks.** This kind of socialization is important and will help build a better business relationship.

SCANDINAVIA

The countries of Sweden, Denmark, Norway, and Finland enjoy some of the highest standards of living in the world and are increasingly important on the international business scene. If you find yourself working with these fine people, here are some tops to get the most out of it.

- **As with Germany, punctuality is highly valued.** Be on time for meetings, for work, events, and for projects and assignments. People tend to show up on time and leave as soon as the gathering is finished. If you will be more than a few minutes late, call and let someone know. Meetings tend to be efficient and get to the point; send an agenda to each attendee beforehand. If you are making a presentation, don't get bogged down with bells, whistles, and flash. State your points clearly and stay on topic.

- **Meetings must always be scheduled in advance,** sometimes weeks ahead of time.

- **A firm but brief handshake is used for greetings,** while maintaining eye contact. In Denmark especially, shake hands with women first.

- **Initially, everyone usually addresses each other with their last name and title,** but it's not uncommon to move on to first names fairly quickly. Take your cues from those around you, but don't initiate. In Denmark, some may start right off by introducing themselves with their first names.

- **The coffee break, known as *fika*, is very important in Sweden.** This is a chance to get to know others, socialize, and take part in an important group ritual. Don't neglect to attend one, even if you're not big on coffee. It's more about the social aspects.

- **Gender equality is important throughout Scandinavia, in society and in business.** For women, this may be quite refreshing. You will be treated with respect and courtesy regardless of who you are, so be sure to return the sentiments.

- **Scandinavians are generally fluent in English,** but be sure to be clear when speaking, especially with complex and detailed proposals or topics, so there are no misunderstandings.

- **Business attire in Sweden and Norway can tend toward the more informal, while it might be a bit more formal in Finland.** Do a bit of research ahead of time to find out what the dress code is where you will be. If you are unsure, normal business attire for women and men is always appreciated and acceptable.

- **In Finland, the sauna is an important part of social life.** Do not turn down an invitation to attend one with colleagues, unless you have a valid medical reason to do so. Long-term business relationships are sometimes established in saunas, or they are used to conclude or continue business discussions. There are no mixed-gender saunas, and you will not be required to be nude, if you prefer a towel or swimsuit, but expect that some people will be unclothed.

- **Despite this comfort with nudity, Finns especially like their personal space,** so be aware of this and don't crowd people or strike up conversations with strangers. If you are invited to a colleague's home, offer to bring a dish or small gift, and be prepared to take your shoes off at the door.

SINGAPORE

Singapore is a unique mixture of Chinese, Malay, and Indian cultures that has adopted many Western features over the past several decades while maintaining its Asian heritage. It's considered one of the best places in the world to do business, so there is a chance you may get to visit at some point. While much will seem familiar, there are some very important differences.

- **Singapore has some very strict laws about certain things:** don't smoke in public places (only in designated areas), don't bring in or use chewing gum, do not litter, and don't jaywalk. While these offenses might seem trivial, violations can result in fines or even jail time. For goodness' sake, do *not* attempt to bring any illegal drugs into the country. This can result in years in jail or possibly even the death penalty.

- **Shake hands with everyone at introductions or the start of a meeting, and again at the conclusion.** A short, firm handshake with a slight bow is normal. Defer to elders and senior members of a group.

- **Offer your business card with both hands.** Accept and examine the ones you are given.

- **Meetings are expected to start on time, with everyone present and prepared.** Being late is a sign of disrespect. Be direct and to the point with whatever topics you are discussing, including money.

- **As with India and the Middle East, do not show the sole of your foot by crossing your legs with the foot resting on the knee,** or use your foot to point at something. Raise your hand in a meeting if you need to get someone's attention and don't point with your finger.

- **Dress codes vary from company to company, but are generally Western-based.** For men, a white shirt and tie, though not necessarily a jacket, are normal, and for women, blouses with sleeves, longer dresses, and trousers are all acceptable. Women may notice some lingering biases against them, though the country has made great strides in promoting gender equality in recent decades.

- **Singapore prides itself on its corruption-free system of business and government.** Gift-giving is not a typical practice in the business world. Be careful about offering gifts, especially to government employees, as it may be construed as a bribe. However, if you are invited to someone's home, bringing a small gift is acceptable and good practice.

- **Developing good business relationships with your Singaporean colleagues can take a long time, even years,** so view your meeting or initial trip as the start of an ongoing process.

- **Avoid discussions of politics and religion,** and if you are traveling with your significant other, do not engage in public displays of affection.

- **Singaporeans sometimes like to bargain when working out business deals.** Don't be offended by this and don't try to make a hard sell to close a deal. This back-and-forth is part of the process. Using the word "no" is kind of unpopular, so you may hear "we'll see" or "I'm not sure" as a substitute. Be prepared for this and don't be offended if it happens.

- **Different groups have different customs when dining.** "Business dinners" tend to be more about socializing and building relationships than conducting actual business. At a dinner with Malay and Indian hosts, avoid using your left hand for eating (it is acceptable to use a fork with your left hand to push food into a spoon, and similar such maneuvers, but don't put the food in your mouth using your left hand). You may be given a bowl of water to wash your hands with before a meal.

THE UNITED ARAB EMIRATES AND ARABIAN GULF STATES

The United Arab Emirates (UAE) and Saudi Arabia are powerhouses of wealth, and many companies around the world are eager to do business there. Culture clash can be a real thing in the Gulf for those not used to the differences, so it's very important to brush up on several topics before going. Here are some of the more important points.

- **The UAE and Saudi Arabia are governed by the law of Islam, known as Sharia.** It is worth your time to read up on some of the customs and expectations in more detail. While freedom of religion is guaranteed in much of the UAE, this is not the case in Saudi Arabia. Avoid discussions about religion and under no circumstances should any proselytizing for other religions (or no religion) be done. This is against the law in both regions and can be punished with jail time or worse.

- **Men should greet men with a right-hand handshake that is light; a firm handshake is seen as a sign of aggression.** Handshakes between men and women are less common. If you are a man, do not initiate a handshake with a Muslim woman, only shake hands if she offers hers first. In some more conservative environments, a woman may offer the edge of her large sleeve to shake instead. If you are a woman, don't offer your hand to a Muslim man to shake. Wait to see if he offers his first. If you are a woman being introduced to a woman, she may offer her left cheek to kiss instead.

- **If you are a man, an Arab man may take your hand to lead you somewhere.** This is entirely normal in Arab culture and you should just go along with it. Men who are close friends will sometimes walk in public, holding hands. This has no romantic connotations and should not be viewed that way. Homosexuality is a sensitive and off-limits topic in the Gulf; don't bring it up.

- **As with India and Singapore, avoid showing the soles of your shoes.** Always remove your shoes if invited to someone's house. The left hand is considered unclean and should not be used in public for anything important.

- **Have your business cards printed with English on one side with the same information in Arabic on the other.** Offer your card, Arabic side up, with your right hand only, and accept business cards with your right hand.

- **Hierarchy and status are important.** People are addressed by terms like *Sheikh* ("chief") or *Sheikha* (the woman's equivalent), and commonly *Sayed* ("Mr.") and *Sayeda* ("Mrs."). Arabs often address people by their title and first name, so James Robertson would be addressed as "Mr. James."

- **Men should wear normal business attire, a shirt and tie. Keep a jacket at hand, though it may not be necessary to wear it. Women should wear conservative attire and short-heeled shoes.** Keep your arms and legs covered, and wear a long skirt, rather than trousers. It is considered polite to wear a scarf over your hair. Do not try to fit in by wearing any traditional local clothing to meetings or events; this will be seen as odd and potentially offensive.

- **Meetings must be scheduled well ahead of time and you are expected to be punctual.** While in theory, lateness is considered rude, in practice lateness is somewhat common, but you should always make the effort to be on time. Perhaps strangely, most meetings at the start of a business relationship aren't especially private, and you may be subject to interruptions and tangents.

- **At a meeting, you may well be offered coffee or tea beforehand, which is a sign of hospitality.** Always accept. Meetings will often start only after a period of chit-chat and beverage drinking. Noninvasive questions about family are acceptable, but if you are a man, be careful about inquiring about someone's female family members.

- **Bringing a small gift is acceptable and a sign of courtesy.** Try to find out something about your host's interests and tailor a gift to match them.

- **At a business dinner, only eat with your right hand.** While alcohol is permitted for non-Muslims in the UAE, it is best to avoid it. Do not ask for it at business dinners, unless your host offers first. Likewise, do not expect anything made from pork to be on the menu. If you are offered more of some food, always accept, even if it's only a little. Your host is expected to pay for the meal.

- **Business relationships develop over time,** so be patient and don't try to force things. Decisions will only be made after much deliberation.

THE UNITED KINGDOM AND IRELAND

The United Kingdom and Ireland will be more culturally familiar if you are from the United States. Even though they have different backgrounds and histories, there is no language barrier (barring slang), and you might feel quite comfortable in London, Edinburgh, Cardiff, or Dublin. There is one important distinction you must remember: the Republic of Ireland is *not* a part of the United Kingdom. The U.K. consists of England, Scotland, Wales, and Northern Ireland. If you are in the Republic of Ireland for business, it's probably best to avoid political discussions altogether.

- **Greetings are done by handshake and friendly eye contact.** Follow the lead of your hosts. There will not likely be any further physical contact. Give people their personal space.

- **Classic business attire should skew toward conservative,** with dark and neutral colors. It's always better to be a bit overdressed. The legal profession in particular tends toward very sharp dress.

- **Be on time for meetings and observe professionalism and courtesy to everyone attending.** Sometimes, particularly in Ireland, other attendees may be a few minutes late, but this is not intended to be insulting, nor is it taken that way. It's acceptable to be a little late for social gatherings. Don't let your voice get too loud, or use overly big hand gestures, especially in business settings.

- **The exchange of business cards tends to be casual,** with no formal ritual or gestures required. Courtesy dictates that you look at the person's card before putting it away.

- **Titles are not of great importance,** and you may find that you move to first-name basis quickly. This is entirely normal and you're welcome to go along with it.

- **Avoid being too direct; it can come off as rude.** Politeness is highly valued, so find a way for disagreement that is more respectful and indirect. Understatement is appreciated; conflict is not. The British tend to say "please," "thank you," and "sorry" more often.

- **The famed British sense of humor can be on display, even in business meetings.** Accept this and have fun with it.

- **Pub culture for socializing is essential throughout the U.K. and Ireland.** You will almost certainly be invited down to the local pub for a drink, and it's imperative that you accept. It's not necessary that you drink alcohol, just choose the alternative beverage of your choice. It is common to buy drinks in rounds, so when your turn comes up, offer to buy for the whole group.

- **In the U.K., it's probably best to avoid certain subjects, unless you are specifically asked your opinion.** These include: the European Union and Brexit, the monarchy (pro or con), the conflict in Northern Ireland, the class system, how much others earn, and so on. Take your cues from what others are talking about.

- **In Ireland, religion and politics are even more volatile topics than in some other countries,** but they will come up in conversation, especially at pubs. Be prepared and if you want to, weigh in. You can, and this won't likely offend anyone, but make sure you are informed about the situation. If in doubt, ask questions.

- **In either the U.K. or Ireland, the weather can be changeable and unpredictable,** so always come prepared for rain!

RESOURCES

While every attempt has been made to provide a comprehensive and up-to-date introduction to the kinds of business etiquette you should know, obviously a book of this size can only tell you so much. If you would like to dive much deeper into the subject (and yes, you should go for it, because there are so many interesting things to learn!), the following books and websites will be amazingly helpful. From successfully schmoozing with your boss to acing difficult foreign customs, from dealing with complex legal issues to knowing your rights, it's all here and much more!

FURTHER READING

Here is a selection of books that go more in-depth about etiquette, manners, business protocols, and good conduct, both at the workplace and elsewhere. There is a lot of great information here, so dive in and absorb it!

Brown, Robert E., and Dorothea Johnson. *The Protocol School of Washington: The Power of Handshaking—For Peak Performance Worldwide.* Sterling, VA: Capitol Book Inc., 2004.

Flannery, Katherine. *50 Essential Etiquette Lessons: How to Eat Lunch with Your Boss, Handle Happy Hour Like a Pro, and Write a Thank You Note in the Age of Texting and Tweeting.* Emeryville, CA: Althea Press, 2019.

Hackman, Richard J. *Leading Teams: Setting the Stage for Great Performances.* Boston: Harvard Business Review Press, 2002.

Johnson, Dorothea. *The Little Book of Etiquette: From the Protocol School of Washington.* Philadelphia: The Running Press, 1997.

Johnson, Dorothea, and Liv Tyler. *Modern Manners: Tools to Take You to the Top.* New York: Potter Style, 2013.

McCaffree, Mary Jane, Pauline Innis, and Richard M. Sand. *Protocol: 35th Anniversary Edition.* Laverock, PA: Center for Protocol Red Book Studies, 2013.

Meyer, Erin. *The Culture Map: Breaking through the Invisible Boundaries of Global Business.* New York: Public Affairs, 2014.

Morrison, Terri. *Kiss, Bow, or Shake Hands: The Bestselling Guide to Doing Business in More Than 60 Countries.* Avon, MA: Adams Media, 2006.

Morrison, Terri, and Wayne A. Conaway. *Kiss, Bow, or Shake Hands, Sales and Marketing: The Essential Cultural Guide From Presentations and Promotions to Communicating and Closing.* New York: McGraw Hill, 2012.

Pachter, Barbara. *The Essentials of Business Etiquette: How to Greet, Eat, and Tweet Your Way to Success.* New York: McGraw Hill, 2013.

Peterson, Brooks. *Cultural Intelligence: A Guide to Working with People from Other Cultures.* Yarmouth, ME: Intercultural Press, 2004.

Post, Peter. *The Etiquette Advantage in Business, Third Edition: Personal Skills for Professional Success.* New York: William Morrow, 2014.

Seglin, Jeffrey L. *The Simple Art of Business Etiquette.* Berkeley, CA: Tycho Press, 2015.

Thomas, Rosanne. *Excuse Me: The Survival Guide to Modern Business Etiquette.* New York: American Management Association, 2017.

Trompenaars, Fons, and Charles Hampden-Turner. *Riding the Waves of Culture: Understanding Diversity in Global Business.* New York: McGraw Hill, 2012.

ONLINE RESOURCES FOR HELP WITH LEGAL ISSUES

Here is a list of websites that offer much more detail on specific topics related to employee rights, harassment concerns, and other legal issues. These sites have extensive amounts of information and should be of help if you need assistance dealing with work-related problems.

Cornell Law School: law.cornell.edu/wex/employment

Equal Employment Opportunity Commission (EEOC): eeoc.gov

Family and Medical Leave Act (FMLA): dol.gov/general/topic/benefits-leave/fmla

Legal Aid at Work: legalaidatwork.org

National Labor Relations Board (NLRB): nlrb.gov

State Labor Offices (listed at the DOL website): dol.gov/whd/contacts/state_of.htm

Unemployment benefits, a guide to collecting by state: nolo.com/legal-encyclopedia/unemployment

U.S. Department of Labor: dol.gov

For more general online help with general business conduct, a search of the term "business etiquette" will bring back more websites than you can read in a single session! Many of them reiterate what is included in this book, and some go into more detail. Searches for specific topics should give you similar results.

ABOUT THE AUTHOR

Tim Rayborn is a writer, educator, historian, musician, and researcher, with more than twenty years of professional experience. He is a prolific author, with a number of books and articles to his name, and more on the way. He has written on topics from the academic to the amusing to the appalling, including medieval and modern history, the arts (music, theater, and dance), food and wine, business, social studies, and works for business and government publications. He's also been a ghost writer for various clients.

Based in the San Francisco Bay Area, Tim lived in England for seven years, studying for an M.A. and Ph.D. at the University of Leeds. He has a strong academic background but enjoys writing for general audiences.

He is also an acclaimed classical and world musician, having appeared on more than forty recordings, and he has toured and performed in the United States, Canada, Europe, North Africa, and Australia over the last twenty-five years. During that time, he has learned much about the business of arts and entertainment, and how to survive and thrive when traveling and working in intense environments.

For more, visit timrayborn.com.

INDEX

401(k), 77, 78, 125

hygiene, 9

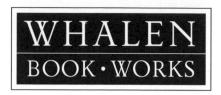

PUBLISHING PRACTICAL & CREATIVE NONFICTION

Whalen Book Works is a small, independent book publishing company based in Kennebunkport, Maine, that combines top-notch design, unique formats, and fresh content to create truly innovative gift books.

Our unconventional approach to bookmaking is a close-knit, creative, and collaborative process among authors, artists, designers, editors, and booksellers. We publish a small, carefully curated list each season, and we take the time to make each book exactly what it needs to be.

We believe in giving back. That's why we plant one tree for every ten books sold. Your purchase supports a tree in the Rocky Mountain National Park.

Get in touch!

Visit us at **WHALENBOOKS.COM**
or write to us at
68 North Street, Kennebunkport, ME 04046